HEAL Y
A RETURN TO
WHOLENESS

THE INTEGRATION OF BODY, MIND, SOUL, & SPIRIT

MICHELLE S. FONDIN

Los Angeles, California

Michelle S. Fondin D.B.A.
michellefondinauthor@gmail.com
www.fondinwellness.com

Publisher's Note: Locales and public names are sometimes used for atmospheric purposes. Any resemblance to actual people, living or dead, or to businesses, companies, events, institutions, or locales is completely coincidental.

Ordering Information:
Quantity sales. Special discounts are available on quantity purchases by corporations, associations, and others. For details, contact the "Special Sales Department" at the address above.

Heal Yourself: A Return to Wholeness/ Fondin, Michelle S. -- 1st ed.
ISBN 9798651123568

OTHER BOOKS BY MICHELLE S. FONDIN

Twin Flame Romance: The Journey to Unconditional Love

Enlightened Medicine: Your Power to Get Well Now

Chakra Healing for Vibrant Energy

Help! I Think My Loved One Is An Alcoholic

How to Run a Successful Yoga Business and Not Go Broke

The Wheel of Healing with Ayurveda

The Wheel of Healing Companion Workbook

There is one unity, unified wholeness, total natural law, in the transcendental unified consciousness.

–Maharishi Mahesh Yogi

Contents

PREFACE   1

INTRODUCTION   5

    What Is Healing?   6

    Must Healing Take A Long Time?   7

    Changing From Object Referral To Subject Referral 8

    Misery Is A Choice   9

    A Return To Wholeness 10

    Introduction: Recap Of Lessons Learned 14

ONE: DISCOVERY OF THE SELF   15

    Suffering Comes From The Self 17

    You Are Not Entirely To Blame   18

    The Layers Of The Self 19

    The Physical Body   20

    The Subtle Body   26

    The Causal Body   29

    The Awakened Self   33

    Chapter One: Recap Of Lessons Learned   36

TWO: THE CONFINES OF THE EGO   37

    The Lens Of The Ego   38

    When The Ego Shows Up As Cruelty   47

    The Usefulness Of The Ego   48

    Getting Bucked By Your Ego   49

    Removing The Confines Of The Ego   50

    Chapter Two: Recap Of Lessons Learned 53

THREE: MOVE BEYOND THE SELF TO HEAL YOURSELF   55

    Dear Self, Meet God   55

Who Or What Are You Living For?   56

Where Is Your Place In The Universe?   58

The False Beliefs Of The Mind   61

Here Are Three False Beliefs Of The Mind: 62

The Soul's Calling   66

Chapter Three: Recap Of Lessons Learned 70

FOUR: AWAKENING TO YOUR SPIRITUAL SELF   71

The Orchestrator Of Events   71

Witnessing Awareness 73

Becoming The Observer   75

Letting Go Of Social Conditioning   78

Daily Practice To Renew Your Connection 79

The Basics Of Meditation   82

You Were Never Born, Therefore, You Can Never Die 84

Chapter Four: Recap Of Lessons Learned 87

FIVE: THE PAST IS YOUR TEACHER, NOT YOUR TETHER   89

What Time Zone Are You Living In?   90

The Past As Your Story 95

The Undoing Of Parental Upbringing   98

Unprocessed Feelings Anchor You To The Past   101

Why It's So Difficult To Process Emotions 105

Rewiring Our Emotional Mind 107

You Get To Decide Who You Are Now   109

Chapter Five: Recap Of Lessons Learned 111

SIX: ACCEPT THE NATURE OF DUALITY   113

Acceptance Of Duality 113

Remaining In Non-Judgment 116

Accept Your Light & Dark Side 119

Pain As Your Guru 121

Heal Yourself: A Return to Wholeness

Your Shadow: A Mask For Pain 122

When A Good Thing Becomes A Shadow 123

Move Toward Pain, Suffering, & Your Shadow 125

Chapter Six: Recap Of Lessons Learned 130

SEVEN: SEPARATENESS TO EXPERIENCE ONENESS 131

How The Awakened Can Take On More Ego 133

The Give, Give, Give, To Depletion Problem 135

Letting Go Of The Need For Approval 139

Chapter Seven: Recap Of Lessons Learned 143

EIGHT: THE RESURGENCE OF THE SELF 145

Going With The Flow Of The Universe Versus Fighting The Current 146

Choosing Sanity Over Insanity 148

Disconnect To Reconnect 149

Nurturing Yourself 150

Self-Acceptance 150

Believe In Yourself 152

Believe In Your Worthiness To Receive 152

Honor Your Inner Wisdom 154

Chapter Eight: Recap Of Lessons Learned 156

EPILOGUE 157

Wholeness As A Way Of Life 157

ABOUT THE AUTHOR 159

PREFACE

All of my life I've been drawn to the concept of healing. Many would say that life doesn't begin here in this current lifetime and based on my pull for ancient healing knowledge, I would have to agree. Ever since I can remember health and healing have been on the forefront of everything I do.

As a spiritual teacher, author, and YouTuber I've been mentoring and coaching students on healing since 2008. Most recently I've published over 150 videos on romantic relationships and in particular the twin flame romantic relationship. A twin flame relationship is like a soulmate relationship on steroids. Everything about it is more intense. As a twin flame, you're led to your own healing journey. Through coaching viewers, the repetitive question has been, "How then do I heal?" In my attempt to answer that question this book came to life.

All of my published books are about healing. Yet, this guide is a little different. Even though I have hundreds of videos published on the subject of healing, I've never published a video series or a book with a step-by-step approach on how to heal yourself.

In addition to twin flames or romantic relationships, I also write and publish about addiction, recovery, and relationships related to healing addictions. All of these topics lead to healing your primary relationship, the one with yourself. While we cannot directly heal others, without consent, we can heal ourselves so that our relationships with others can move to a higher level.

Most of my healing came as a result of two relationships since 2013. Throughout much of my adult life I had been called to work on healing, especially since my experience with cancer in 1999. Yet the deepest healing came when first, I encountered a relationship with an alcoholic, and secondly when I met my twin flame. I cannot emphasize enough that much of this growth came with an enormous amount of pain. For many years I didn't realize that through relationship I was called to heal. I simply looked at it as torture or payback for bad karma. In addition, I blamed myself for consistently choosing the wrong men or being too broken to choose the right ones. About halfway through my relationship with the alcoholic, I began to realize that much of the experience was about *my healing* and not his. Then, when I met my twin flame and saw that many of the triggers from the previous relationship began to show up, I started to put the pieces together.

When you're in a painful situation and more importantly in painful relationships it can be easy to either blame yourself or point the finger at the other person. In my case, I did both until I learned the bigger lessons. To help you realize your capacity to heal yourself I'm going to gently lift you out of both of these thoughts and into another one altogether. The process of my own healing came when I realized that I didn't need to blame myself or the other person, and that I wasn't being punished. Instead these relationships were designed to help me heal myself and return to my sense of wholeness. Your pain may not come out of a relationship, per se, but from a situation that has been a constant struggle. With that said, I often find that even the most difficult situations come with various relationships attached to them. For it is through relationship that we learn the most about ourselves.

In coming out at the tail end, I now realize the beauty in all of these struggles. Through them I learned how to dive deep into my darkest fears. And in the end I found my true self. Through the experience of my healing journey, I hope to teach this process to you. While your story may be different, the process through the human psyche is much of the same. We all live the same stories in different forms. We all gather wounds from our past and live immersed in some level of self-doubt. We share similar insecurities and feelings of inadequacy. To sum it up, we all tend to feel a little broken. The variance to the road to healing comes with the amount of time spent on a specific lesson. We all have certain areas of focus that need extra attention. Mine may be different than yours, but the road carries us forward all the same. Plug in your story to the part of the healing journey that feels right for you.

One thing is for certain; by the end of this book you will feel empowered and liberated from the confines of yourself. If there is one thing to know, it's that we all have the power to unlock our own healing. Once you realize this, you are already free.

Let's explore the journey into healing together, shall we? But in order for this to work, you must *do* something. You have not picked up a sit back, relax, and enjoy the book, book. This book is designed for you to get to work. You will need to ponder, dig, and dive deep into the depths of who you are. You will need to get honest and authentic with yourself. Now is not the time to pull the wool over your own eyes or to applaud yourself for being a better person than the next. It's time to look at yourself in all of your vulnerability that is raw and unappealing. You will need to face your inner demons and darkest shadows. Get ready to get down and dirty so you can come out clean.

The best way to enjoy this healing journey is to keep a daily journal of your findings. Be the scientist on the quest of discovery. Write down everything that arises. Next, you must have a daily meditative practice or your healing journey will take much, *much* longer. I teach and adhere to a mantra-based meditation practice. But you can use mindfulness, guided meditation, prayer, breath observation, or nature walks. The only thing I highly recommend, regardless of your meditative practice, is to spend at least 15-20 minutes per day in total silence. The ideal, however, is to spend 30 minutes twice daily in total silence. Here's why. As you begin to uncover the layers of your wounds, you will need time to sort them out. You may have an incredible discovery in the middle of the day, while working, but it may not be the appropriate time to dive deep into it. Silence gives you the time to take the mind where it will go. It allows for peacefulness amid the storm. Throughout this book we will shed light upon the other benefits of a consistent meditation practice.

Get ready to get busy. As in my other books, I would wish you luck, but luck is not what's needed. Healing yourself requires embracing the journey full on. You hold the key to unlocking your power to heal. And that, my friend, requires no luck, but rather courage and strength. Be courageous, be strong, and surrender to the process. Namaste.

INTRODUCTION

The word *heal* comes from Old English, which means "whole." Therefore, healing is a return to wholeness. This definition of the word "to heal" resonates with the belief system that I've taught for over twelve years, and that is the healing system of yoga. The word *yoga* comes from the Sanskrit word *yuj*, which means "to yoke" or "to join together." In the practice of yoga, which goes well beyond physical postures, we join together the body, mind, soul, and spirit. In other words, we become *whole* or we heal.

The process of healing involves reuniting all the aspects of ourselves that have been partitioned. When we feel unwell, in any part of our lives, it's because we have a sense of not being whole. Every part of us calls for reuniting and that is why we feel uneasy until we experience oneness. Most people search their whole lives for this feeling. Few will ever attain it. Many will have momentary glimpses into what it feels like to be whole at key moments in their lives. For example, the feeling of falling in love and being united with another can give you the sense of wholeness. Oftentimes women who experience the euphoria of looking into their baby's eyes for the first time after giving birth feel united in being.

In reality, the sense of not being whole is but an illusion. We are already whole as we are, though we fail to realize it. In order to illustrate this example, I'm going to take you on a journey beyond the confines of the physical.

At one time you were one, united with your Source. You can call this source whatever you choose, God, higher power, higher self, or universal sprit. Upon arriving here on Earth you received a human body, which includes a piece of universal soul as well as your individual soul. In truth, you are constantly tethered to Source or God. It's simply the arrival into human existence that causes you to forget.

To recap, we are united with Source, we are born, and then we forget we are still united with Source. This is where partitioning happens. We begin to not only feel separate from our Source, but then we also begin to feel separate from everyone else. And because of the perception of separation, we then begin to feel separate from ourselves.

In reality, the *only* thing we need to do is to remember. We must remember that we are not separate from God, but that we are united and always have been. Right now you must be thinking, *Michelle, that is easier said than done.* Throughout the years, we've raveled ourselves into a great, big ball of confusion and it takes some doing to unravel it. And that is where these teachings come into play.

To heal yourself, you must first remember that you are united with your Source and are therefore perfect and whole. After you've established that truth as your anchor, you're ready to gather up the pieces of your partitioned self and bring them back to union.

WHAT IS HEALING?

In the Western world, when we focus on healing, we often refer to the physical body. We try to eat well, exercise, take supplements, or do whatever we can to maintain good physical health. For some, healing means taking a pill. For others, it means not having to take any pills. And yet for many, healing is only a focus when illness arises. You get the flu or a cold and remain aware of what you must do to regain physical health for a few days or weeks. Then, once you start feeling better, it's back to normal life. When we feel anywhere from mediocre to good physically, we tend to not place too much awareness on healing.

Several of my published books including, *The Wheel of Healing with Ayurveda* and *Enlightened Medicine*, have many chapters on physical health. In this book, our focus is on another realm of healing, which is to discover your ability to transcend suffering by learning the reasons for it. Therefore, our focal point is on emotional, psychological, and spiritual healing. The beauty of the return to wholeness is that when you heal a few aspects of yourself, physical healing often follows.

MUST HEALING TAKE A LONG TIME?

Modern living tells us that healing takes a long time. Healing takes as long as you want it to take. Many people sit in psychotherapists' offices for decades rehashing details of the past. Most spend a large portion of their lives repeating the same painful lessons time and again, while refusing to see the bigger picture. Somewhere down the road they say, "Hey, why are these same things always happening to me" Or for example, "Why do I always date the same person in a different body?" That's because instead integrating the lessons when all the red flags show up, most people turn a blind eye with the thought, *Oh, it will be different this time.* And when it isn't, they get angry, frustrated, and erect walls.

The human mind is genius. If you want to, you can integrate the lessons of healing at a quick pace. All it takes is a decision. You can decide for example;

- Do I want to wallow in my pity? Or do I want to live in the present and appreciate all that I have?
- Am I going to curse my past? Or am I going to look at it as necessary for my learning and growing?
- Am I going to wait for this person to change? Or am I going to step up and live my life now?
- Am I going to hold a grudge? Or learn to forgive and move on?

You can decide now to make those changes. You don't have to wait for some magical moment or a set number of sessions in the therapist's office.

CHANGING FROM OBJECT REFERRAL TO SUBJECT REFERRAL

In order for healing to occur, we must change our focus. Our entire lives we are called to focus on objects outside of us for recognition of our wellbeing. Without a doubt, it all started when we were babies looking to our caregivers to see if we were safe. Have you ever watched a baby hit his head and then look to see his parent's reaction before starting to cry? It's almost as if he's waiting to see, if it's serious enough to warrant tears. Oftentimes when the parent reacts with a cheerful, "Oh, you're okay!" The baby will start to play again without a fuss. But if the parent says with a worried tone, "Oh no baby! Oh no, oh no! Are you okay?" The baby will immediately start crying.

Even though we're adults now, we often do the same. Let's say you lose a job you hated. Then you call five friends and tell the story about how you lost your job. Afterward, you prod to get their reaction, "That sucks right? Doesn't that really suck?" And if one friend says, "Yeah, that sucks!" You get angry and upset. But if another friend responds, "Well, didn't you hate that job?" You sigh and say, "Actually, yes. I really hated it. Now I can look for a job I like." Do you see how we are continuously looking outside of ourselves to see how we're doing?

In the same way, many are looking outside of themselves for happiness and fulfillment. They truly believe that if they get the better job, the great lover, or the fabulous car, they'll be happy. When they get all of those things, they might be happy for a time. Then the job gets boring, the lover cheats, and the car gets a big dent and they are sad again.

Others think, *If the people in my life would just do A, B, or C, then I'll be happy.* Let's say you want your boyfriend to propose. And the fact that he's not proposing is making you miserable. Or if your mother, the drunk, would just get sober, all of the family reunions would be much better. Making your happiness dependent on the actions of others is giving away your power to be happy. In the end, you will always be suffering because no one in this world is ever going to fulfill all your desires the way you want. Someone is always going to fall short.

It's time to turn the switch from object referral to subject referral. You now get to decide on your own happiness. And you get to decide when and how to end your suffering. Of course a big part of this teaching is to surrender to your higher power and to get in touch with your spiritual self. But you will no longer be dependent on any earthly person, place, animal, or thing to bring you to your place of joy and peace. Your place of joy and peace will be within.

MISERY IS A CHOICE

No matter what your circumstances are, misery is always a choice. Nelson Mandela, the leader of the movement to end South African apartheid, was imprisoned for 27 years but he came out in 1990 with a positive outlook and firm resolve to his cause. Many survivors of the German Nazi concentration camps survived because they made the decision not to live in misery regardless of the injustice of their imprisonment. People from all walks of life and in every socioeconomic status have managed to choose happiness and contentment over misery.

In this book you will learn how to end your suffering and heal yourself. But you have to make it a conscious choice. You have the right to your own misery. And you have an equal right to your own happiness. By the end you will possess the tools. You only need to make the choice.

A RETURN TO WHOLENESS

Throughout this book I will emphasize and re-emphasize a return to wholeness for healing. The fragmented parts of yourself must be reintegrated if you want to experience a return to health.

Let's take, for example, your physical body. Modern medical science wants us to believe that it is separate from us. You must go to a doctor to tell you how your physical body is doing. How can you *not* know how your physical body is doing? You live with it at every moment. You make choices as to how to feed it, hydrate it, and how often to give it rest. *How could you not know how it's doing?* Yet we've been taught, by outsiders who don't know us, that we don't know how our body is doing and whether or not it's healthy. If you really think about it, I mean, *really* think about it, that's absurd! It's completely and utterly absurd! Societal conditioning has taught us to be 100% disconnected from our bodies so that we rely on others, known as experts, to tell us if our bodies are doing well. How in the world did we get here?

Heal Yourself: A Return to Wholeness

It's no wonder you're suffering if you can't even trust your inner wisdom about your own body. Some people even talk to their body saying, "Oh, you better not get sick!" Or "I wonder if you have a disease or cancer..." as if it's some sort of mystery. Others play Russian Roulette with their body. They go to the doctor for a checkup (to see how their body is doing), then they get a clean bill of health according to the few measurements that Western doctors assess. After the yearly checkup, they treat their body like a fun house until the next appointment. They drink, smoke, overeat, forget to sleep, and then sweat it out for days before their next checkup and pray that their body is okay. Then they go to the "body expert" for the verdict. The disconnect between body, mind, emotions, and soul is so great that they haven't a clue.

You might be thinking, *But Michelle, disease does exist. And many diseases are unseen.* That is true. And I'm not undermining the fact that proper diagnoses of certain illnesses are necessary for early treatment. However, I would like to teach you to become so integrated in yourself and so aware that you won't need an expert to tell you you're doing well. Disease always comes with pre-signs and signs. Most people are unaware. In my other books, including *The Wheel of Healing with Ayurveda* and *Enlightened Medicine Your Power to Get Well Now*, I go in depth on the stages of disease. I also mention how constant testing can lead to unnecessary medical procedures. Your body is a healing machine. It's literally designed to heal. When something in your body isn't able to be healed, it will let you know. You just have to pay attention. And in order to pay attention you must have a fully integrated mind, body, soul, and spirit.

Most diseases are 100% preventable. The 5-10% that aren't are up to God or the universe. We can't understand fully why some diseases occur. For that, we have to trust in God's plan. For disease prevention, which I do address in many of my other books, you are called to do your absolute best in taking care of your integrated self, but the rest is up to Divine order.

One of my greatest teachers and mentors, Dr. David Simon, lived a stellar life health-wise. In addition to being a trained neuro-surgeon, he practiced as an Ayurvedic practitioner and meditation teacher. He had practiced Transcendental Meditation since medical school and became vegan around the same time. He designed his life around serving others, healing, and teaching others to heal. He was a bit of a perfectionist and had a fast temper when it came to his students, but that was only because he had high standards. At age 59, Dr. Simon self-diagnosed his own brain tumor. I was sitting in a Chopra Center meditation retreat in 2010 when I heard him tell the story. He explained how he was backing his car out of a parking space and side swiped another vehicle that he didn't see. He said (I've taken the liberty to paraphrase here), "Being my own neurosurgeon, I immediately did peripheral vision tests on myself and noticed that I couldn't see out to one side. I ordered my own CAT scan for the same day." Dr. Simon was diagnosed with an aggressive form of brain cancer. While he had a lot of money to fight the brain cancer, he passed away from it in 2012.

When I heard that he had lost his battle to brain cancer, I was dumbfounded. Dr. Simon knew all of the ancient and modern healing techniques and had lived a stellar life. *Why did this happen?* I kept asking over and over again. It almost didn't seem worth it to strive toward a perfect lifestyle if something could happen like that to take away your life so suddenly. After a long time of pondering, it hit me. We all come into this world with a terminal illness; we are born knowing that we're going to die. We just don't know how or when. Dr. Simon lived his life to the best that he could. And he lived a great life. He was vibrant and healthy up until his diagnosis. He lived to help and serve others. He had great friends and a wonderful family with amazing kids. As far as I knew him, he lived each day to the fullest. He lived as an integrated being so much so that he was even able to diagnose his own brain cancer when it happened.

Healing yourself does not mean you'll live pain-free or that you will never, ever suffer. The reintegration of the self or the return to wholeness means that you will be able to live out most of your days in great vitality and freedom from disease. You will have the vibrancy to live out your life purpose, dreams, and have a positive impact on others. In your fully integrated self, you will be more ready and willing to serve a higher purpose and live joyfully more days than not. Healing yourself means you are free.

INTRODUCTION: RECAP OF LESSONS LEARNED

1. Healing means a return to wholeness.
2. Our focus in this book is on yoga's definition of healing, union, which means the integration of body, mind, emotions, soul, and spirit.
3. You were born whole. Human life is the process of remembering.
4. Healing is as easy as a decision.
5. The process of healing is a recalibration from object referral to subject referral.
6. 90-95% of all diseases are preventable and curable.
7. Healing means living a life full of vitality and freedom from disease most of your days.
8. Healing yourself means you are free.

ONE

DISCOVERY OF THE SELF

In order for you to return to wholeness, you must have a vision of your true self. How can you pick up the pieces of your partitioned-self if you have no idea who you are in the first place? Many of us have been caught up in the game of object-referral for so long that we forget who we are and that includes our true nature and desires. It can be scary when you come to this realization. I know many moms who stay at home to raise kids and when their children reach adolescence or even earlier, when they enter school, these moms have a major identity crisis. In talking with them they say things like, "I've been somebody's mom for so long that I forget who I am." I was in that place at one time.

I had a baby while I was still in college. Because I grew up with a controlling parent, I was completely lost as a college student. That being said, I *knew* what I wanted to do early in my life. But as you may have experienced too, having a parent tell you that you can't have your own desires creates a lot of internal conflict and confusion. So there I was, at age twenty-two and utterly confused about my place in the world. I wasn't in the location I wanted to be in, and I wasn't doing or studying what I really wanted to study or do. Then I found out I was pregnant. At the time it gave me a sense of purpose and identity. I could be somebody's mother and I knew I would do it well. During my pregnancy I had an enormous amount of love for my baby and I anticipated that being a mom would be even better. And it was. But I awoke suddenly in my mid-thirties with three kids and an extremely unhappy marriage. I had forgotten Michelle, and who I was. It was an awful feeling. In the midst of becoming a mother and playing out that role, I had completely cast aside myself as an individual. I had morphed into what someone else had expected of me. And it felt like death. I had left the 22-year-old girl somewhere in the past and for fourteen years I had ignored her, leaving her out in the cold. She was sad to have been left behind. And as a result I was sad.

Recreating myself took years. The growth that should be a normal part of your early twenties had to be repurposed for me, then, with the responsibility of three children. In rediscovering myself, I learned something that I had known all along; being a mother was a huge part of my identity, but it wasn't the whole picture. In addition, I learned that I had many gifts and talents that had remained latent, just waiting to be developed. It wasn't until I left my marriage, that I truly began to unfold into the person God wanted me to become. Even so, it wasn't until over a decade later that I had the courage and strength to let go of everyone's preconceived notions of the person *they* wanted me to be. I believe my last piece of true liberation, into forming my true identity, was when I moved to California on June 29, 2018.

When you are living someone else's hopes and dreams for you for most of your life, the re-identification of the self can be scary. So much is unknown. In transforming into the person I wished to become, I had to think back to who I was before I had kids. I had to explore, *What were my hopes and dreams exactly? Who was I back then?* The partitioned or fragmented parts of myself were pieces I had voluntarily given away to my mother, father, and husband at the time.

In finding out who you are, you'll have to gather back the pieces of yourself that you voluntarily gave away. Remember, you always had a choice.

SUFFERING COMES FROM THE SELF

Even though you might believe that your suffering comes from others, such as your parents, spouse, or boss, in reality, the source of your suffering, for the most part, is yourself.

Your belief system about what should be or shouldn't be and your expectations of others and yourself all contribute toward your suffering. For example, you might wish that your mother would have treated you differently and now you're going through years of therapy to "undo what she did." In this, you're holding onto the belief that your childhood could have been different and that the outcome of who you are today would have been better based on this belief. That may or may not be true. But you're making yourself miserable by imagining another outcome, instead of living for today. Here's another example. You're expecting your spouse to change to match something that might fulfill your needs and desires and you're miserable while waiting for him to change. Again that suffering is coming from you and *your* expectations of what should be. Rather than accepting that you married a person who may never match your needs, you're awaiting with misery the magical day that he transforms into another person.

When you think about most situations that make you suffer, it boils down to two things: not accepting what is or refusing to change your situation to be able to accept what is. That's it. Once you understand that concept, you can move toward the "why" of your belief system. By and large, your belief system largely determines how fast you heal.

YOU ARE NOT ENTIRELY TO BLAME

I say those words with the greatest amount of affection. In order to raise little humans with a notion of self-respect, compassion, and love for the self and others, we need adults who possess these same notions.

If in raising children, the point of view is from the ego, then ego-consciousness will be transferred. You can't expect children to learn how to have good self-esteem and how to respect themselves and others unless they have role models who teach them these principles. Yet in recent years I have seen the pendulum swing from one extreme to the other.

I was raised in the old-school way of parenting. Parents were the authority figure and as a child you did what you were told. No one cared about your opinions. You had to obey blindly whether you liked it or not. If you wanted a sense of self-esteem, you had to toughen up and find it yourself. Depending on your personality you either sank or swam. Many people I grew up with defied authority and got in trouble. Others turned to sex, alcohol, or drugs to cope. I was somewhere in the middle. In fact, it wasn't until I had my epiphany around age 36 that I realized how low my self-esteem had been when it came to interpersonal relationships. I attribute that in part to my upbringing with the constant message that I had to listen to others and not trust my own instincts.

When my generation started raising kids, many of us swung the other direction completely to overcompensate. We did everything for our kids. We inflated their sense of self-esteem. The parents who were raising kids at the same time as me seemed so traumatized by the way they were raised that they always put their kids first. They signed their kids up for many activities, volunteered in classrooms, and catered to their kids' every need. And as a result, many kids now have a sense of entitlement or an inflated sense of ego. As for the parents, they have become depleted in resources and energy and they are still denying their own needs. Where is the truth in parenting? My guess is that it's somewhere in between.

It's important that we teach kids emotional intelligence. But it's equally important to teach personal responsibility. Self-respect does not come from people artificially inflating your ego. It comes from earned results of hard work and higher-level behavior. And the best teacher is when a parent or caregiver shows children through example when they take care of themselves first.

THE LAYERS OF THE SELF

The way we've generally been taught is to have a constricted view of who we are. We say things like, "This is just the way I am. Take it or leave it." Or for example, "I'm like my father and that's the way he is, so I guess I'm just hardwired that way." Throughout years of training we impose limitations on our lives. I'm here to help you shatter all of that.

It's true that certain aspects of your personality or genealogy are indeed inherited. In addition, everyone has learned traits that are hardwired during childhood. However, the body, mind, and spirit combination, that makes up wonderful you, is more fluid than you think.

Vedic philosophy has a detailed explanation of the layers of the self. Let's broaden our view of who we are through this ancient wisdom.

THE PHYSICAL BODY

The first three layers according to ancient Vedic texts are in a subset called the physical body. These three layers are the body, environment, and energy body.

YOUR PHYSICAL BODY

The physical body is composed of roughly 37.2 trillion cells according to an article in Smithsonian Magazine from 2013.[1] Your cells are in constant flux. They are growing, changing, and regenerating. Human cells are also in constant motion. The human body vibrates at a frequency anywhere between 5-10 Hz.[2] (Planet Earth vibrates at 7.83 Hz.) Therefore, the notion that the human body is a fixed object is simply not true.

Most people believe that once you hit forty, the body only degenerates. They even say things like, "It's all downhill from here." Nothing could be further from the truth. The body is a well-programmed machine that responds well to change for the better and for the worse.

Right before I turned 49 (Yes, I'm almost hesitant to say I'm forty-nine.), I noticed my body was getting flabby, I mean, it got really flabby. The flabbiness did not reflect my mostly vegetarian

1   "There Are 37.2 Trillion Cells in Your Body." Rose Eveleth, Smithsonianmag.com. October 24. 2103. Page accessed on March 4, 2020, https://www.smithsonianmag.com/smart-news/there-are-372-trillion-cells-in-your-body-4941473/

2   "The Hippies Were Right: It's All About Vibrations Man!" Tam Hunt. ScientificAmerican.com. December 5, 2018. Page accessed March 4, 2020. https://blogs.scientificamerican.com/observations/the-hippies-were-right-its-all-about-vibrations-man/

and sometimes vegan diet or my fairly active lifestyle. Upon doing some research I found that after age thirty women lose 5-8% of muscle mass per decade. That muscle loss also increases more rapidly after age sixty. Muscle-loss, called *sarcopenia*, can be reversed with proper and consistent weight training and increased protein intake.[3] Seeing my body turn to jelly made me extremely anxious as I never considered myself as actually getting older. Doing cardiovascular exercise alone wasn't helping. In fact it was hurting my muscle mass. Since you lose fat and muscle during intense cardio sessions, you must make up for the muscle loss by including intense weight training in your regimen.

In order to reverse the muscle loss, I started a hypotrophy weight-training program four days per week. I also included branched-chain amino acids (BCAA) supplements in my daily diet and increased my protein intake. For eight weeks I stopped intense cardio exercise and focused on my hypertrophy training. When I added back my cardio exercise on week nine, I was feeling better and stronger. I'm pleased to announce that the flabbiness is gone. My body is firmer and has better muscle tone than when I was in my twenties. My weight-training program taught me that the body truly is malleable and can be taught to reverse aging.

The same goes for the human brain. While the human brain starts to shrink after age thirty, we can still create new neuropathways. Neuroscientists have found that the brain has neuroplasticity even as we age. You can increase cognitive ability as you "workout" the brain by learning new skills and even by meditating daily.[4]

---

3   "Muscle Tissue Changes with Aging." Elena Volpi, Reza Nazemi, and Satoshi Fujita, Current Opinion Nutritional Metabolic Care, January 12, 2010.

4   "How the Brain Changes with Age." Alexis Wnuk. BrainFacts.org. August

When it comes to healing disease or healing symptoms that can lead to disease, you must embrace the notion that your body *can* change for the better. So even though you were raised with the notion that the human body is a firm physical form, I hope you're starting to see that a solid or rigid body is the opposite of reality.

THE ENVIRONMENTAL BODY

Often overlooked is the influence of the environment all around you. The environment includes anything that extends beyond your physical body. This can include your home, car, and workplace. It also includes the people who surround you. A greater extension of your environment includes the geographical location where you live: your neighborhood, city, state, county or country. I love the Vedic expression that goes; As *is the microcosm so is the macrocosm.* The opposite is also true. As *is the macrocosm so is the microcosm.* In other words, even though you may not perceive it, your environment defines you to a certain extent. If your outer world including your home, car, or office desk is in chaos and disarray, it means you have a certain level of internal chaos that must be worked out.

After I separated from my then husband in 2008 and brought my three children and two cats back to the United States from France, I tried to bring about a sense of normalcy for my kids. I was just starting my career as a yoga business owner and in addition, I tried being the full-time hands-on mom I had always been. But being alone with three young children while trying to start a business took its toll. Furthermore, I had no prior business experience and had little idea what I was doing. For many years I had been a stay-at-home mom. And while the job was difficult, I didn't have to

30, 2019.

worry about being the main source of income. Starting in 2008, I had to make it a priority. Even though I felt I was holding it together relatively well, certain aspects of my children's behavior showed that I wasn't. One of the things I wanted to do was to ensure that all three kids kept their normal level of extracurricular activities. To that end, I found a piano and voice teacher to give lessons to my two older children. After several weeks, the teacher remarked that my middle child wasn't progressing at all. She said it was almost as if he was living in a household filled with chaos that didn't leave room for a disciplined practice. At the time I took great offense to this comment. While she may have been largely overstepping her bounds, (After all, my middle child was only 9-years-old at the time and playing piano was hardly his top priority.) she had a point. I only realized the truth of her comment years later. The truth was, my home was chaotic. I was trying to take on way too much. Not only was I going through a divorce, but also raising three children alone. I had tried to maintain the schedule of a stay-at-home mom while starting a business and doing part-time work to make ends meet. It was too much and it *was* chaotic. My middle son had to babysit his younger brother often. A clean home or car was absolutely last on my list of priorities. The environment we were living in at the time affected us all.

The environment as your extended body means you don't live in isolation even if you live alone. We are interdependent on one another to live and thrive. How you treat every environment you inhabit affects everyone else and vice versa. Grasp this idea fully and you'll be able to awaken to a deeper respect for your extended body.

THE ENERGY BODY

The Western world hasn't paid much attention to the concept of the energy body for a large portion of our modern times. However, I believe we're becoming more aware. Vedic philosophy calls the energy body, *prana maya kosha* in Sanskrit. *Prana* means vital life force. Life force exists in every living thing. You can be alive and not have much prana. Prana gives vitality and vigor.

In the West we measure our days by our energy. We say things like, "I'm feeling tired. I need a coffee." Or "I'm overworked." Or even, "I'm feeling lazy." As in all the layers of who you are, the energy body is integrated with the physical body. If your physical body isn't fed high quality food and clean water, you will feel lethargic. Additionally, if you don't exercise your physical body, you won't feel the presence of the vital life force within you.

The energy body is also your aura or "vibe." Have you ever noticed that you can *feel* a person's vibe as they walk into a room? That vibe is their energy body. Your energy body is strengthened not only by care of the physical body, but also by a healthy emotional body, mind, and spiritual body. It's sort of like your DNA imprint. The energy body cannot lie. It tells the tale of who you are before you can even say a word.

In connecting the environmental body to the energy body, it's important for you to note that your energy body picks up remnants of energy from those around you. Therefore, if you're constantly hanging around negative people, even if you're not a negative person yourself, your vibe will radiate negative energy. In the same way, if you hang around places with low vibrations such as inner-city nightclubs or strip clubs, for example, your energy body clings onto some of that energy and carries it along with you.

Heal Yourself: A Return to Wholeness

For a long time I didn't know the importance of discernment when it came to whom I let into my inner circle. In fact, it took me decades to learn. Especially in dating relationships, I often frequented men who had low vibrations. They were negative, possessive, addicted, or just plain mean. Being someone who is naturally positive and uplifting, I always thought I could "help" them or offset some of that negativity with my positivity. But that's not what happened. Instead, being in their constant presence brought me down. Somehow the ions of negativity stuck to my positive energy field and caused me to be more negative, sad, and frustrated. Furthermore, my positivity didn't necessarily cause them to be more positive; it only served as fodder to power their increased negativity. It was strange. Now I'm very careful. I only let positive and uplifting people into my inner circle. In addition I know that I can't just give away my positive energy for free without an equal exchange.

Before we move on to the next layer, I want to emphasize one point here. Notice that in the example above I said the words, *inner circle*. Your inner circle includes the people who are closest to you such as immediate family, a significant other, and two or three close friends. Your inner circle is generally small. They're usually the people with whom you spend a majority of your free time. I am not saying that it's good to live in a bubble or refrain from helping others who are in need. In fact, it's best to be a light for others. Spread your positivity and aim to create a higher vibrational impact for the world. But when it comes to your inner circle, be careful whom you chose to let in.

When it comes to healing your energy body, many techniques exist to clear it and keep it healthy. We will go over some of these techniques in subsequent chapters.

THE SUBTLE BODY

The next set of layers, called the *subtle body*, is comprised of the mind, intellect, and ego. These three layers reflect restriction when it comes to ascendance into enlightenment. Most of the world's population lives from the perspective of the subtle body. You've likely heard the expression, "You're living in your head." That expression is a direction reflection of subtle body involvement. Living at the lowest levels of being, the mind and intellect are servants of the ego. If I were to take a pop culture reference of Disney's *The Little Mermaid*, the villain Ursula would be the ego and the two eels, Flotsam and Jetsam, would be the mind and the intellect. In many instances, the mind and intellect can move into higher level thinking where the thoughts and reasoning come from spirit. However, if the ego is not tamed, then more often than not, the mind and intellect serve to prove that the ego is right. Let's now explore each of the layers in the subtle body.

THE MIND LAYER

Boy, oh, boy, does this layer give us problems. The crazy mind, the monkey mind as you might call it, thinks thousands and thousands of thoughts a day. According to the National Science Foundation in 2012, the human mind thinks anywhere between 12,000 and 50,000 thoughts per day.[5] Whichever way you interpret that, by the hour, minute, or second, that's a lot of thoughts. It's no wonder so many people suffer from anxiety. They can't seem to escape the noise of their own mind.

5   "The 70,000 Thoughts Per Day Myth?" Neuroskeptic. DiscoverMagazine. com. May 9, 2012. https://www.discovermagazine.com/mind/the-70-000-thoughts-per-day-myth

Heal Yourself: A Return to Wholeness

The problem most people encounter when it comes to the mind is that they believe they can't do anything about it. Those who suffer the most from anxiety don't want to sit in silence because they fear their mind. That's why they medicate with alcohol, drugs, or prescription pills. They're afraid of themselves.

The mind is you. It's a part of who you are. And since you're in control of you, you can control the mind to some extent. But since you haven't been taught, you must learn just like any other skill. We don't have classes in school that teach us how to manage the part of us that thinks thousands of thoughts per day. Religion doesn't even teach us that. Therefore the anxiety comes from the uncertainty of, *Where is my mind going? It feels like it's going insane!* It's not going insane, you just haven't learned to manage it yet.

The other day I was coaching a group of students in a meditation course. I was telling them that the mind is like an untrained puppy. If you've ever seen a puppy walking with its owner, it will look at anything in front of it. Newly discovering sights, smells, and tastes, that puppy will move toward anything it can and change directions every few seconds. No one looks at the wandering puppy and says, "Bad puppy!" No, they know that this puppy is young and untrained. The nature of the puppy is to discover its world and it doesn't know that it must not eat paper or sniff the inside of a trashcan. But if the owner doesn't take the time and effort to train that puppy, it will become an unruly dog. The mind is the same. The nature of the mind is to think thoughts. It's not bad. It's just untrained. You, the one who is in charge of the mind, can train it.

A great emphasis in this book will be on healing the mind. It's not something that is easy to learn, but with discipline and consistent practice, you can shift your focus from fear to empowerment.

THE INTELLECT LAYER

The intellect layer is the part of the subtle body designed to judge and discern. It's a necessary part of who you are. You must learn how to judge and discern to keep safe. Modern psychology and religion tells us that we must not judge. However, a certain level of judgment is important to be able to cope with life. The softer word for judgment is discernment. To carry out your life mission, you must be able to intellectualize morals, for example. As you form your moral boundaries, a sense of judgment is present. Why do you adopt certain morals? Whose morals were they? Why do these morals resonate with you? Why don't other morals resonate? How far will you let your morals stretch before breaking them? All of these questions move you to judge what is right for you and your life. Without it you tend to float around with no sense of a stance on anything. Then you are inclined to adopt a mindset of "anything goes." Without a sense of judgment, killing is neither right nor wrong. The same goes for stealing. Understand that the intellect with judgment and discernment are necessary. Judgment will also tell you for example, "Don't get into a car with that guy. Things could go wrong." Or, "I know I'm allergic to shellfish, so I won't order crab for dinner."

I'm also fully aware that the intellect layer gone wrong can cause you to do things like judge so harshly that you disregard others based on exterior or superficial factors.

Notice in the descriptions for each layer that positive and negative aspects exist. You will then be able to see the potential genesis for poor health and also the direction you can take toward healing.

THE EGO LAYER

Being that the ego is the most constricted part of who we are, I'm dedicating an entire chapter to it. Suffice it say that along with the mind, great challenges come with the constriction of the ego. Like all the other layers, the ego is absolutely necessary. Be wary of authors and speakers who say it's not. The sticky wicket is being able to tame the ego into a reasonable size and allow it the space to play, but within limits. An untamed ego is also a great source of human suffering. But again, as in all the other layers, it is completely pliable and able to be sculpted and molded into something beautiful.

THE CAUSAL BODY

The last three layers make up the *causal body*. Included are the individual soul, the collective soul, and the universal soul. In these layers we move beyond the body-mind into the ethereal.

THE INDIVIDUAL SOUL LAYER

As we progress into the more esoteric layers of our existence, we begin to notice the "me" that was always there. There exists a "me" who has never changed from your birth, to your childhood, to your adolescence, into young adulthood and to where you are now. That self, who you remember as you, is the individual soul layer. One of my favorite teachers, whom you will hear me quote often, was Dr. Wayne Dyer. He used to say, "Have you ever said out loud, 'The other day I was saying to myself...?' Who is 'myself'? And who is the 'I'? That indicates two people. The 'myself' and the 'I'." Now whether or not the first one indicates the mind, the ego, or even the intellect is up for debate, the second one definitely denotes the unchanging self, the spiritual self.

Your individual soul is a repository of all of your life experiences. It holds your purpose and life mission. It is the part that connects you to all other souls as well as to your Source. Your individual soul is the unchanging part of you that inhabits your physical body for the duration of this lifetime. Depending on your belief system, the individual soul also carries impressions and memories from other lifetimes. Additionally, it can carry karma from your past and past lives to be balanced in this lifetime.

In exploring the notion of healing, we will continually emphasize the importance of the individual soul as your touch point. Again, as in the "training of the mind", we don't have school for soul training. Religious organizations would like us to believe that rituals and doctrine help make us aware of our soul, but I am quite certain that most don't actually teach us how to access the soul.

In this explanation, I'm not discounting the importance of religion. I wholeheartedly believe it has a place and purpose. If we dismiss religion and say, "It's too this or that," we're ignoring the fact that many people need parameters and boundaries to manage living in this world. Additionally, religion can provide glimpses into your personal soul as well as connection to Source. However, in my upbringing as a devout Catholic and now as a non-denominational Christian and in my study of other world religions, I have not seen that the world's major religions teach us how to directly access the personal soul. It wasn't until I studied Eastern philosophies, and more importantly yoga philosophy, that I was able to fully understand how to differentiate between the individual soul and the other parts of me.

By the end of this book, you will also have a deeper look into your individual soul.

THE COLLECTIVE SOUL LAYER

The other day I was coaching a man who, on the outside, seemed to have everything. He migrated to the United States from Africa when he was seventeen and now, in his mid-forties is a successful surgeon. This man came to me because he had just put in his resignation and was troubled by what the future held for him. He was worried about money, career, and his love life. Upon hearing his story it dawned on me. It doesn't matter who we are, where we come from, or where we stand in society. We are all concerned about the same things. We all want stability and certainty when it comes to job, home, love, and family.

The stories of humanity have been repeated over time. And that is the collective soul. We have much to learn from the people who have lived before us. Their stories and energy are here to help. I have a particular fondness for Walt Disney. When I'm feeling down or find that I'm not living up to my own expectations, I turn to his life story for inspiration. We can find strength in others' stories of struggles and triumph and we often do.

Inspiration from the collective soul can bring us up, but it can also pull us down. In today's world of immediate communication, news travels at lightening speed. But so does the tribal mindset. The power of the collective can destroy or help.

In late 2019, my 16-year-old son, told me about one of his favorite YouTubers, Mr. Beast, who was raising money to plant 20 million trees. A donation of one dollar would plant one tree. My son turned to me and said, "How much are you going to donate Mom?" I donated on his and my behalf. But the most beautiful outcome of the collective is that within 55 days, the campaign raised $20 million to plant 20 million trees. That is one example of how the collective soul can come together to uplift the planet and world consciousness.

Sometimes this world can feel very lonely. But in reality, we are never alone. When I was doing research for my book, *Help! I Think My Loved One Is An Alcoholic,* an alcoholic in long-term recovery gave me the following advice: *When you're feeling self-pity or that you're all alone in the world, get out there and help a stranger. Do something for someone else. And you will feel less alone.* That is a beautiful illustration of the collective soul.

THE UNIVERSAL SOUL LAYER

The totality of everything that exists makes up the universal soul. It's the heartbeat of the entire universe. In the universal soul exists a universal flow to all things. You are a part of that universal flow. You might be programmed to think that this is a rat race and that you must fight your way to get ahead. But the reality is, you are already a part of the perfect dynamic flow of the entire universe. The plan for you and your life is just as perfect as the plan for everything else in it. Healing is about remembering that fact and discovering your part. Suffering comes in part by the belief that the universe is not perfect as it is.

In Ayurveda, the medical branch of Vedic wisdom, there is a concept called *pragnyaparadha,* which means "mistake of the intellect." Ayurveda teaches that *pragnyaparadha* is the source of all suffering and disease. The intellect wants us to believe that we are individuals on this Earth but not interrelated or connected. It also causes us to believe that we are separate from our Source and the flow of the universe. In this mentality, we must forge our own path. Furthermore, the mistake of the intellect causes us to believe in our fragmented self. Armed with this false belief, we put all the pieces of ourselves into separate boxes. For example, we go to a doctor to take care of our physical body, then to a psychologist for our mind, and then onto a pastor for our spiritual self. Pragnyaparadha wants us to believe that each facet is separate and therefore must be treated separately. When in truth, each and every layer of who we are is integral to all the other layers. And the highest truth is that the wholeness of who we are, is completely integrated with life itself.

THE AWAKENED SELF

Thus, when we talk about the self, which part would we be referring to? It sounds a little insane doesn't it? Do we say I'm speaking from my ego, my body, or my soul? Do we entertain the notion that my body is feeling hungry or that I'm hungry? All of these concepts can make it sound like a bunch of new-age, spiritual mumbo jumbo. These descriptions are not designed to make you go crazy. They're here to show you an expanded version of you. You were already all of these things. My outline simply showed you these various aspects. Awakening is synonymous to awareness. My expansive description of the self broadened your awareness, hopefully.

The question that remains is, "Why do we need this awareness?" The answer is we need this awareness to understand who we are. We need this awareness to understand that we have all of these layers of existence, but that we are not bound by any of them. To say, "I'm the ego," is not the entire truth. Nor is it entirely true to say that I am a soul. I am all of the layers without being one in particular. It might be easier to understand if you think about the roles you play in life. You might play the role of a mother, sister, daughter, spouse, or someone who works or plays poker. You could be a father, son, cousin, best friend, someone who runs marathons, and bakes a mean cake. But none of those singular roles defines you as a whole. They are all a part of you and you might even act differently based on the role you're playing. However, let's suppose you stop running marathons, that wouldn't shatter the holistic aspect of who you are, would it? In this example, some people might get stuck with the notion that if they can't run marathons anymore, it takes away their entire identity. And that is where suffering begins.

Now, go back to the layers of yourself. With awareness you come to an understanding that you possess all of these layers. You have a bird's eye view of awareness that sometimes you can be in the layer of the physical body, other times in the intellect, or in the ego. Suffering comes when you identify with one too strongly. In my previous example, I shared my fear about being in my forties and losing muscle mass. I could have remained in suffering if I had said to myself, *That's it! I throw in the towel. I'm just going to be weak and old from now on.* Do you see the ridiculousness of that supposition? Yet, people do that all the time. They take one aspect of the self, identify with it, and therefore, stay rooted in suffering.

The enlightened one says, "I have all of these layers, but my identity is none of these. My one true self is beyond space, time, and causality. It has no definition, but flows with the energy of the entire universe." And when you come back to earthly living from that enlightened place you can now say, "I know I am at times the ego, mind, intellect, soul, the collective, and the physical body. I enjoy them all and to live fully is to embrace them fully." Then you live out the aspects of yourself in the present moment as fully as you can. Bring awareness to what you're doing at all times so that you can make the best choices for you and for others. But live fully in all of them.

For example, if you're having an ego day, have an ego day. Above all have it be the best ego day you possibly can. Make everything about you without harming others. So if you want to have your cake and eat it too, do that. Buy two pieces: one to eat and one to take home. In a fully aware ego day, you're going to tell others joyfully, "I'm going to be playing out my ego today, love it or stay away. But that's me, today."

The same goes when you're living your intellect layer day. You might be debating with people and arguing your points until the cows come home. But do it joyfully and with awareness. Furthermore, a mindful person in the intellect layer also hears others out and enjoys their arguments too. It's all part of the fun.

As you may be starting to see, the awakened self doesn't live in a cave meditating all day while donning a halo. The awakened self lives mindfully and aware and enjoys life in the present with every aspect of the self. And that is how you begin to transcend suffering and heal.

CHAPTER ONE: RECAP OF LESSONS LEARNED

1. The true self is an integration of all of your layers, which include: the physical body, environment, energy body, mind, intellect, ego, individual soul, collective soul, and universal soul.

2. Ignorance of your true nature generally comes from an upbringing that doesn't teach children the nature of the self.

3. You are not any one layer of your existence, but can play different roles based on the dominant layer for a time.

4. Bring full awareness to all aspects of yourself to live fully and in the present moment.

5. *Pragnyaparadha* is a term from Ayurveda Vedic philosophy that means, "mistake of the intellect." The mistake is that every part of yourself is separate and that you are separate from everyone else and your Source.

6. The enlightened being knows that the true self exists beyond space, time, and causality, you were never born and therefore, can never die.

TWO

THE CONFINES OF THE EGO

The physical ego serves as its own worst enemy when, by delusive material behavior, it eclipses its true nature as the ever blessed soul. —Paramahansa Yogananda

In the previous chapter I mentioned that the ego is a very special part of the self. To make our egos feel extra special, I have dedicated an entire chapter to the ego. Look who's smiling now!

In my meditation course I teach that the ego is a necessary part of who we are, but it's also the most constricted part. It's necessary because it's our form of outer expression in the world. The ego differentiates "you" from "me." The ego is important when you want to get a job or win over a potential lover, for example. You have to possess the wherewithal to prove that you're a better candidate than the next person. And that takes a little ego to accomplish.

Everyone has an ego. The amount of ego expressed will vary from person to person and according to the situation. The major issue with the ego, when it comes to healing, is that it can get in the way.

THE LENS OF THE EGO

Most of us for most of our lives have been trained to look at life through the lens of the ego. Since most societies operate through ego-based means, we are surrounded by ego consciousness everywhere we go. Being that we don't tend to have other examples of non ego-based behavior, it becomes difficult to understand how to act differently. In every part of society, ego-based behavior is constantly reinforced. But just as it's hard for you to know why you speak your native language well, it's a challenge to look outside of the lens of ego when it has always been there.

The lens of the ego, if we were to translate it into key phrases, looks something like the following examples:

I need to get what's mine before someone else does.
That person offended me on purpose.
I'm insulted.
You don't love me.
People are assholes.
You don't deserve me.
How dare they say that to me!
I'm right.
You're wrong.
It's us versus them.
You should see things my way.

The ego is interested in one thing: the survival of the self. To that end, the ego is constantly on the defensive, is fearful, and looks to others as a threat. The ego tries to make the person it's attached to look better, stronger, smarter, and more appealing than others.

Looking through the lens of the ego, the person behind it believes that they are the center of the action and sometimes the center of the whole universe. For example, a person caught up in ego will say things like, "See those people over there? They're talking about me, I know it!" Or they might be self-conscious about what they're wearing by saying, "I know I shouldn't have worn this. People think I'm stupid." They truly feel that everyone's world revolves around them.

People living through the lens of the ego...

- Make others feel bad to boost themselves.
- Often criticize others.
- Get offended easily.
- Get angry, impatient, or irritated frequently.
- Measure their success based on comparison to others.
- Have to consistently "beat" others in any sort of challenge.
- Talk about themselves and their accomplishments often.
- Can't understand why everyone doesn't see things the way they do.
- Tell others how they should be living their lives.
- Try to make others feel guilty about not communicating with them or seeing them more often.
- Try to run the show for themselves and everyone around them.
- Are frequently intolerant of others.
- Have trouble seeing things outside of their perspective.
- Expect others to adapt to the things they want.

- Have a narrow perspective about how life is and how it works.
- Believe that others are living to serve them.
- Have the need to be right all the time.
- Argue frequently with others to "prove a point."

Let me emphasize that every single person on this planet has an ego. You are not spared of an ego and neither am I. However, the degree to which we see life through the lens of the ego makes all the difference. Many people can only view life this way. For others, the ego lens is where they see life most of the time. Before we explore how to defocus the ego's lens, let's take a look at other ways in which the ego tends to rule.

THE NEED TO CONTROL

No matter which way you slice it or dice it, controlling behavior is always a part of the ego. Remember that the ego's main need is survival. And if the ego feels unsafe, it's going to try and control variables to make it feel safe again.

Record this one fact, the more controlling someone is, the more fearful they are. They are living in deep fear, ruled by the ego that says, "I feel so out of control and unstable that I must control others to regain stability."

Everyone is running their own race. Each person has a life path and purpose that they must live out accordingly. If you find that controlling behavior has been an issue for you in the past, you might have noticed that you try to tell others what they're doing wrong and how they can do it right. You might get angry when others don't follow your advice. Or you might get upset when they don't do things on your timeline. Control can also surface as little jabs or insults when a loved one doesn't live up to your standards. It may come out as passive aggressive remarks such as, "I told you so." Or "You should have listened to me or you wouldn't be in this situation."

I grew up with a very controlling mother. She not only micro-managed my environment and told me everything I was doing wrong much of the time, but she also constantly checked up on me. As a result, I learned how to lie to her early on. I also got a car as soon as I turned sixteen to escape her controlling behavior. Then I ended up marrying a man who was equally controlling, but in a different way. He used insults and criticism to try and maintain control. In addition he used stonewalling and threats to leave the marriage if I didn't do what he wanted. After years of being controlled, some of this controlling behavior rubbed off on me. When I found myself in a relationship with an alcoholic in 2013, I tried everything I could to control the situation. Later I learned that I couldn't control him, the drinking, or the situation, but I could control my reactions and myself.

In the end, people who try to control others have a difficult time controlling themselves and their own lives. They feel unsafe and have a hard time trusting. They live in fear of many things including not being loved, being abandoned, or not being accepted. When these very basic human emotional needs are threatened, the ego shows up in big ways.

The way to deal with others who are controlling is to show them that they are loved, but to set a boundary so they can't continue the controlling behavior. For example, you might say something like, "You're afraid that I don't love you. I do love you, but it's not okay to look at my emails without permission. We need to respect each others' boundaries."

If you find that you have been controlling with others, examine the basic emotional needs that aren't being met in your life.

Are you afraid of someone leaving or abandoning you?

Are you afraid of someone not loving you if you show vulnerability?

Are you afraid to share your true feelings?

Do you feel trapped in a relationship and feel that the only way to manage the situation is to try and control it?

Are you afraid to leave a relationship?

Are you afraid of not being needed or not being important in someone's life?

Are you afraid of losing that person?

Do you feel your life is falling apart and by controlling others around you, you have a feeling of keeping it together?

Does controlling another person in your life by "helping" them constantly make you feel better about yourself?

People who try to control instill fear in the other person by threatening to take away one or more of the most basic human needs.

Here are some basic physical human needs:

Food, water, shelter, safety

Here are some basic emotional human needs:

Love, appreciation, acceptance, acknowledgment, affection, peace, trust, respect

Heal Yourself: A Return to Wholeness

Here are some basic spiritual human needs:

A sense of purpose, a feeling of belonging, being part of a community, freedom to express connection to a higher power, play or creative time

Let me give you some examples to show you how we, being in an ego mindset, can try to control.

The wife who is a stay-at-home mom with four small children under the age of six refuses to have sex with her husband on the basis that he doesn't help out more around the house. While this may be a valid point of frustration, she is trying to control by taking away his need for affection, love, and acceptance.

The parent who takes away friend play dates for two weeks because their child came home with an average report card. That parent might be disappointed that the child isn't doing better in school, but he or she is trying to control by taking away the child's need for acceptance, community, and playtime.

The ego thinks it's doing better or knows better by "punishing" those who don't do as it wants. But in the end the need to control others only brings about more pain and strife between people.

THE PAIN OF THE EGO SELF

Since we are hardwired for survival, most people live in the ego self first. The ego self is trying to get its way and come out on top. That's why it's important to the ego self to be right. The struggle to prove your point or to be right can be exhausting. Furthermore, it causes pain to yourself and others along the way.

It's easy to see the ego's struggles for survival when you turn on the TV or look at some of the most viral videos on the Internet.

The other day I was at a nail salon getting a pedicure. In the course of my fabulous spa treatment, a TV screen in front of me played a couple of different talk shows. While I don't remember the titles of the shows, the premise was the same for both. The host comes on and introduces a person who is now going to be confronted by another person such as a sister, spouse, or significant other. During the show they're going to argue and try to prove who is right and who is wrong. The host acts as an intermediary or instigator, depending on the show, and adds fuel to the ego flare up for all involved. For me, it's painful to watch. These shows are examples of humanity at its worst because they are all slaves to their ego self.

Whilst living in the midst of the ego self and operating from it, with little to no awareness, you are living in pain. Someone is either not doing enough for you or is doing you wrong. The paranoia is constant, as you must keep tabs on who thinks what of you and what you think of others. With this ego pain you never live in peace.

The ego self is constantly one-upping. You know this if you've ever watched the innocence of small children at play. Younger children have not yet adopted something we call the "social mask" or socially filtered behavior that makes the ego look a little better behaved. So if one gets a green Popsicle the other will scream, "Where's my green Popsicle?" And when these small children get on the swings one will shout, "Look at me, I'm swinging higher than you!" And the other will respond, "No, I'm swinging higher than you! Look!" And so it goes. Little egos are constantly competing between themselves. Then we get older and it's not so cute. But we still behave in the same way and the problems become bigger. Instead of, "I want a green Popsicle like you," it becomes, "Oh, you slept with my husband! Well, I'm going to sleep with yours then."

Healthy competition and healthy doses of ego are necessary in certain circumstances, as I have emphasized. But think back to your most painful moments in arguments with others. It's likely that you were both acting from the standpoint of the ego. You were hurting so you wanted to hurt. Or you were wronged so you wanted to get back, at least in words. Trying to "teach someone a lesson" is also ego. Even saying, "See, I was right," in the case that you are right is still pushing the ego's agenda.

Of course everyone jokes from time to time. And good rapport between friends can help lighten a mood that becomes too serious or somber. Every person needs to be given a reality check sometimes and a loving relationship can be a place to do this. But it has to be loving and kind and not because you want to prove your superiority.

One game I've started playing with myself when it comes to "giving advice" to others (I put that in quotation because while I may be thinking it's advice, it just might be my personal opinion.) is by asking, "Will I create more negative karma by what I'm about to say or do?" When I think about karma in the Eastern philosophy sense, it means action. But that action can create a positive, negative, or neutral effect. Each time you create something negative with your actions, including your words or even body language, your karmic debt must be repaid. At this point in my life I'd like to avoid creating negative karma. Usually if you're about to create negative karma, your ego self is involved somehow. By asking yourself, "Am I about to create negative karma?" it helps to keep your ego in check.

ANGER AS MASKED HURT

Anger is not my go-to emotion. My go-to negative emotion is either anxiety or frustration, which in turn are usually a result of feeling out of control. Yet, one day recently I found myself angry about a particular situation that I thought I had laid to rest. Being a deeply reflective person, I decided to take a look at the anger. In a journal I outlined the reasons why I was angry. The verdict: it was clearly the other person's fault. With that conclusion my ego was greatly satisfied. But even that conclusion, although I was correct in my assessment, didn't remove the anger. I have great love for this person and it didn't sit right that I should still be angry. The following day I did a Reiki healing meditation for me and the other person combined. Here's what came up. In the meditation I found myself explaining to this person what I wanted him to do and say, instead of what had happened. And then the defining moment was revealed. I wasn't angry with this person. I was hurt. I was hurt that he didn't respond differently. I had interpreted his response to mean that he didn't love or care about me. And that hurt. Once I was able to pinpoint the hurt, the anger dissipated.

In reality, most people are not that self-aware. It may sound as if I'm patting myself on the back and I am in this case. For once, I got it. And that is something I can celebrate.

The truth is; anger in all cases is masked hurt. Usually this hurt is based on one or more needs not being met. For me, the needs in the previous example were the needs to be loved and accepted.

EXERCISE:

To be able to get rid of anger, you must uncover the reason for the hurt. An easy way to do this is to go back to the conversation or situation and relive it, but in a different way. Since you are the director this time, write out the script. What would you say? What would the other person say? How would you act? How would they act? What would the conclusion look like? As you go through this exercise, you will be able to unravel the point at which you became angry and the moment before is where you felt hurt. Then go through which of your needs weren't being met at the time. It's a great way to release pent up anger and hurt and move toward love and forgiveness.

WHEN THE EGO SHOWS UP AS CRUELTY

If emotional pain continues to stay unprocessed it can show up as either depression or cruel behavior. We are all aware of kids in school that showed up as bullies. They would steal other kids' lunch or lunch money, make fun of kids for the clothes they were wearing, or steal their ball on the playground. It seems that there was one in every class. Now kids and adults have to deal with cyber bullying.

When you dig deep into the reasons a person makes the decision to be cruel toward another, you can usually see that they have major self-esteem issues. Those self-esteem issues generally came from being teased as a kid or by having a controlling or cruel parent or older sibling. Sometimes it's revealed that they were abused as a child or had to deal with family members with substance abuse problems or mental health issues.

Cruelty comes out as layers and layers of pain stacked one upon the other that has never been addressed. In recent years, many people are categorizing others, who have cruel ego-based behavior, as narcissists. Rare is the true narcissist. According to the *Diagnostic and Statistical Manual on Mental Disorders*, between 0.5 and 1 percent of the general population is diagnosed with Narcissistic Personality Disorder.[6] A true narcissist is not able to show sympathy or empathy at all. It is a person who is so caught up in ego that they are unable to change points of view. Some people, however, may show extreme narcissistic behavior, especially when they act in a way that is mean-spirited toward others.

Generally speaking, you must avoid the person who has reached the point in pain where their actions or words come out as cruelty. The cruelty can show up as emotional, psychological, verbal, or physical abuse. You need to protect yourself first. By trying to change them or match their behavior by being sarcastic or verbally abusive only adds to their pain and to yours. Remember, the ego's mission is to survive. And a person who is experiencing that much emotional pain is constantly getting the signal that they are not surviving. That is why they lash out. To illustrate, let's compare a cruel person to a wounded tiger or bear. Approach them and they will hurt you. If you have tried to recommend they get psychological help and they have refused (not the tiger or bear, but the person), then your job is to protect yourself. You can love them from afar.

THE USEFULNESS OF THE EGO

I've spent most of this chapter ego bashing. However, I started the chapter by telling you that the ego is necessary. It *is* necessary. In fact, most highly sensitive people or spiritually aware people might have an issue with not having enough ego. They are afraid of hurting others or stepping on others' toes. So they skulk around and

6   "Is Narcissim Common? The Answer May Surprise You." Tanya Peisley. Sane.org. March 20, 2017. https://www.sane.org/information-stories/the-sane-blog/mental-illness/is-narcissism-common-the-answer-may-surprise-you

let others walk all over them. That is the other side of extreme behavior.

You need your ego to assert your will and to set boundaries. The ego delineates where you end and others begin. In order to have good self-esteem and self-worth, you need to be able to set healthy limits. If you find you have an underdeveloped ego, chapter seven will help you mindfully use the ego to develop a healthy sense of personal power.

GETTING BUCKED BY YOUR EGO

Growing up I watched many Looney Toons cartoons. In those days cartoons were relatively simple and tried sometimes to teach children a sense of right from wrong. To that end, a character's moral dilemma was often played out by a debating devil on one shoulder and angel on the other.

I feel the ego's plight for dominance over the spiritual self is similar. Since most societal norms include ego-based socially acceptable behavior, it can be difficult to choose higher-level behavior. Let me give you an example of one ego-driven socially acceptable behavior. Among males, in general, it's socially acceptable and almost expected that they watch pornography. It's almost like a rite of passage. I've heard male friends and companions joke around about watching it commonly. There seems to be no question as to whether or not it's right or wrong. Nor does the question arise, "Is this self-centered behavior?" If you were to really decode it, the behavior objectifies people and trivializes the sexual relationship. The fact of watching it makes the person choose quick pleasure that satisfies the ego and buys into an industry that exploits others. It's got ego-dominance stamped all over it. Yet, for men in particular, it's considered weird if they don't partake in this activity. Many men are chastised by their friends for taking a stance against porn. Do you see where this is going? It's almost an easier choice to watch it, admit it, and let your life be normal according to the other people in your tribe.

One show that I got sucked into watching with my middle son is *The Bachelor* series. We even ended up doing a podcast together for one season. It was a fun show to watch with him. But eventually it got too painful to watch because of the ego games the contestants played with one another. For the most part, the Bachelor or Bachelorette is serious about finding love. Yet they have to contend with some contestants who are only participating for the television exposure. When you see what is popular on TV and streaming services, it's hard to try and live out higher-level behavior. There just aren't many examples to follow today.

When you allow yourself to stay trapped in ego-consciousness, you are in pain. You can rarely experience peacefulness. The ups are very high and the lows are rock bottom low. Most ego feelings are generated by external forces. That is why you experience little to no internal peace. Ego-consciousness is always dependent on others or external situations. It's true that others can affect you. Furthermore, your behavior also has an effect on others. However, the single track of the ego won't allow you to experience anything else.

REMOVING THE CONFINES OF THE EGO

Notwithstanding the truth about the ego, this book is about healing. We've clearly denoted that following in the footsteps of the ego is not going to release your pain. Therefore, let's look at how we can move away from the ego and live more from our higher self.

The first step in removing the confines of the ego is to recognize the voice of the ego and continuously bring awareness to it. You cannot remove that which you do not know. In fact, this is the major problem for most people. They are not able to see the behaviors of the ego from a distanced point of view. So they fall prey to the automatic reactions that the ego dictates. The question then is, *How do you notice or bring awareness to the ego?* For the remainder of this book we will explore how to get into *witnessing awareness* in order to access your spiritual self. It is only from this point of view that you can clearly determine which behaviors, including internal dialogue, are from the ego and which are from higher-level awareness.

With that noted, however, you must not stay fixated on ousting the ego like an unwanted houseguest. If you do this, the ego will only grow stronger. You must become aware that the ego is a permanent part of your self and that you can only loosen its constricted hold on you and your life. What I've noticed is that the best way to overcome ego constriction is to welcome it in, but in a modified way. Become aware that the ego has its place and allow it to have a voice when appropriate. Let me give you an example. In a job interview, you must point out all the ways in which you are a better candidate than anyone else vying for the position. That can only be done from the point of view of the ego. Another example is when you're dating and you must "show your best self" in order to woo a love interest. In that case, the ego isn't the only part of you that comes into play. However, if you go into a dating scenario without any ego, for example, you won't come off as being as self-confident or self-assured as you could. Remember that in these two examples we often only have a small window of time to display our outer personality and our ego self is a great way to give it a boost. Yet this only works if it's done the right way, through the integrity of our higher self.

Therefore, when you overcome the confines of the ego, you become the master of the ego. The ego no longer has a hold on you. And when I say *you*, I'm speaking of your higher self, which can be interchanged with the term "spiritual self". As you move to this new place of being, you can start the process of healing.

CHAPTER TWO: RECAP OF LESSONS LEARNED

1. Everyone has an ego and you can't get rid of it while you're still alive.
2. Most of us have been trained most of our lives to live through the lens of the ego.
3. The ego's need is to keep you alive and therefore, its mission is survival.
4. While the ego is the most constricted part of who you are, it's necessary for certain aspects of life.
5. Ego dominance causes people to try to control others.
6. Fear is the ego's biggest emotion.
7. Bringing awareness to the ego and its related behavior is the first step away from it.
8. When your ego is "ruling the roost," it's impossible to live a life without pain.
9. The way to tame the ego is to become the master of the ego through your spiritual self.

THREE

MOVE BEYOND THE SELF TO HEAL YOURSELF

If you want to know your true nature, you must have yourself in mind all the time, until the secret of your being stands revealed. – Nisargadatta Maharaj

Healing can start to occur when you begin to get out of your own way in order to heal. But first, you must make a connection with your higher power. Some call this higher power God, while others call it spirit, universe, or Mother Nature. (For the sake of simplicity, I will refer to higher power as God.) It doesn't matter what you name your higher power, it's only essential that you recognize it. The idea is that you are surrendering to something greater than yourself with the knowledge that you don't know enough to understand the dynamics of the entire universe.

DEAR SELF, MEET GOD

Many people are allergic to the word "God." When they envision the meaning of God, they are flooded with memories of their religious upbringing or rigorous dogma that was punitive in nature. Other people, who did not grow up with a concept of God, might see that people around the globe fight in the name of God. Still others have grown to learn and accept that God and religion are two different things. Together religion and God can create a supportive and loving environment for some, but don't necessarily have to go together to embody the belief.

Direct experience creates your relationship with God. Once you have the experience of God, no one can take it away from you. In that experience, you have touched upon the divine essence that lives within you. In the modern world, many people miss the mark because they are either looking for God outside of themselves or they are allowing others to interpret their meaning of God for them. Those of us who have had direct experiences with God have noticed similar traits. When you experience God you feel humbled. You feel grace, love, joy, humility, and gratitude. Furthermore, you can feel warmth and comfort. Oftentimes the experience of God is accompanied with great emotion and many tears.

WHO OR WHAT ARE YOU LIVING FOR?

Since you now understand that you're hardwired for survival and that the constant battle to stay alive is a great source of suffering, it's important to change your focal point. People who experience the most joy and the least amount of suffering have a focal point on serving others and a higher power.

I must emphasize that you must take care of yourself first in the way of ensuring that all of your basic physical, emotional, psychological, and spiritual needs are met. It goes back to the overly used but true expression, "Put on your oxygen mask before helping others." You are of no use to others or to God if you're not getting proper sleep, exercise, and nourishment.

Now that I've acknowledged your responsibility to yourself, who or what are you living for? Are you living for your ego, for your family, or for your community? Are you living to make all the money you possibly can or to increase your social status? Why are you here? What is your purpose? Who do you serve?

You must get clear on that. Who you serve and whom you live for determine most of your actions and behavior in life. For example, I know people who live for Fridays. As a result they put in their time at work and do the bare minimum to get by. Additionally, they might complain about their circumstances at work or at home. But when Fridays come, they have pep in their step and impatiently await the five o'clock hour. They party it up over the weekend and then do it all again the following week. It might sound cliche, but how many people do you know in that category?

Then I know people who are living for retirement. They might be in their fifties, sixties or maybe even younger. They talk and dream about how many years they have left before retiring. When they speak, you can hear the excitement in their voices as they talk about their future plans.

Few people live in the present moment. And even fewer have a clear vision as to their part in the bigger picture. Even those who say that they are here to live for God might not feel peaceful about God's plan for them. We need to learn to surrender and listen as each moment unfolds.

The combination of living in the present along with serving God are necessary to move through life peacefully. At the same time, it's not about living in the present alone. I know many people who live in the present but who live for alcohol, drugs, shopping, gaming, or gambling. Those are not people who transcend suffering. But neither are the people who live for Fridays or for retirement alone.

So what does it take exactly to be able to have a clear vision? And what does it take to feel your integrated self in the present moment and know what you're supposed to be doing in life? The answers lie in understanding your place in the universe and by listening to your soul's calling.

WHERE IS YOUR PLACE IN THE UNIVERSE?

The integration into wholeness comes more easily for those who understand their place in the universe. I've been studying illness and wellness for over twenty years and one thing I've come to notice is that those who have compelling reasons to live and be well heal faster and live longer. When these compelling reasons are fully in place, it doesn't matter how many times they get sick or how many diseases they contract, they always seem to pull through. Then there are those who don't understand their place in the world or who have lost their zest for life. For these people, a simple cold could lead to death.

My father is not an example in health, but he is a leading example in healing. While I'm not certain of his compelling reasons to live or how he views his place in the universe, he has a strong will to live. For 35 years my father was a smoker and recreational drinker. At age 47 he had his first heart attack and angioplasty. To date, in the year 2020, he has had seven cancers, a stroke, a quadruple bypass surgery, and a kidney transplant. He has issues with high blood pressure, type II diabetes, obesity, and a carotid artery that is 95% blocked. According to medical science, he should already be dead ten times over. But when he reached age 75, three years ago, he told me joyfully, "I've signed up for another 25 years here." And that was when he was battling stage 4 colon cancer. Today my father is 78 and while he's not healthy by any standards, he believes he has a place here and that is giving him a reason to be alive. He is a living example that your hardcore belief system supersedes any medical diagnosis.

In my book, *The Wheel of Healing with Ayurveda,* I tell the story of my friend's mom who battled ovarian cancer with a less than 30% chance to live, twice. The first time she was told she had less than six months to live. The second time, the ovarian cancer came back as lymphoma and had spread to her entire body. Doctors told her that they had never seen anyone beat that type of cancer twice. However, this 4 foot 11 inch spunky Irish woman was not going to let cancer beat her. She has five children and many grandchildren. As I was growing up I looked up to her because she was the fun mom always involved in everything. She volunteered at all school events, threw great parties, and was always upbeat. While I've been out of touch with the family for a couple of decades, my mom just showed me a picture of her at a barn party that she threw with her entire family and neighbors at age eighty-four. The picture showed her dressed in tight jeans and cowboy boots while line dancing with her sisters and friends. She has outlived her husband and is now living her life to the fullest.

Given these examples, I ponder the question, "What gives some people an incredible drive to live and others a lackluster view of life?" Furthermore, "What makes people move away from suffering toward healing and others move toward suffering for recognition and special treatment?"

I believe much of this mental focus has to do, in part, with your vision of your place in the universe and your role in the bigger picture. I have always had zest for life. Yet, I wasn't always healthy. In fact, I grew up being sick most of my childhood. But I always had the will and desire to be healthy and made it the focal point of my entire life. My mom has had an entirely different view of life. I remember about ten years ago I said something in front of my mother that was a bit insensitive, but not intentionally. We were waiting for a bus to unload some wheelchairs and I said, "I will never be in a wheelchair." My mom, mortified, said, "How can you say that? Don't say that! You don't know that." And with full confidence I responded, "I just know it." As I said, it probably sounded callus. After all, the person or people in the wheelchairs didn't ask to be handicapped. But that wasn't my point. My point was that I believe I can create my own destiny including the will and desire to remain healthy. My mom believes what most people do and that is, *the human body degenerates with time.* I have adopted the belief that it doesn't have to be that way. You can choose to increase your health and wellbeing as you age. Additionally, suffering is optional.

Why are we afraid to ask for what we want when it comes to health and strength? Somehow we've been conditioned to believe that we can't ask for wellness. We've also been conditioned to believe that we can't assume wellness as if it's our human right.

I believe the underlying tone in my mother's voice was, "Don't tempt God. He just might punish you if you say you'll never be in a wheelchair." The supposition in that statement is that God is just waiting to dole out punishments to those who declare health as a human right. Unfortunately, many believe this to be true.

Heal Yourself: A Return to Wholeness

If you believe you have an important role to play in this lifetime your inner drive will be solid. Your will to live and heal will not be based on fear, but on something bigger than yourself. When you are living to help and serve others and in essence also serving God, your body does everything to move toward healing. It's an invisible force that moves through you that no one in the medical field can explain. Numbers and statistics mean absolutely nothing when it comes to the invisible force known as meaning, purpose, and the will to live.

So what is your role in the bigger picture? Why do you believe you were placed on planet Earth at this moment in time? What compelling reasons do you have to live and stay healthy? Are you just a speck of dust in this infinite universe? Or do you believe that you have a great role to play?

While these questions can create uneasiness when you don't know the answers, it's best to explore them sooner rather than later so you can find your compelling reasons. You don't have to be a great inventor, a CEO, or a high-powered person to feel you have a great role to play. Every role is needed and it's your belief system about your role that determines your thinking. In addition, your roles will morph and change as time goes on. You must keep a vision of your purpose throughout your lifetime to keep zest for your life *and* your health.

THE FALSE BELIEFS OF THE MIND

Mind is consciousness, which has put on limitations. You are originally unlimited and perfect. Later you take on limitations and become the mind. —Ramana Maharshi

Even if you have a clear vision of your place in the universe, you must stay flexible, as the only constant is change. Many people get stuck in the belief that *who they are* is a fixed thing. When you remain fixated on the notion of who you are and of your place in the universe, when it's time to change, you can experience more suffering. An ancient Vedic saying goes, *Infinite flexibility is the key to immortality*. Meaning, if you stay rigid like a metal pole, you will miss out on many opportunities for life fulfillment. But if you bend like the palm tree in the wind, you are much less likely to break. Life is much better for that palm tree that bends in times of adversity. It snaps back and is more resilient after being tested.

However, society tends to have certain expectations. When we're young we have a tendency to follow the path laid out before us. Let's take the example of a young student who wants to study law to make a difference in the world. That student does well in high school, gets into a great college, and tells everyone he's going to be a lawyer and make a difference. He then graduates at the top of his class and attends the best law school in the country. After two years of law school, shocked and disappointed, he discovers that he doesn't like studying law and that everything he's worked toward is not pointing him toward what makes his heart soar. Fixated on his previous goals, he pursues and graduates from law school and passes the bar. But as he pushes through he notices that he's more and more unhappy as time passes. How many of us can relate? We tend to look at our lives as a straight line instead of a messy web that can take us in many directions. Usually the pathway to your destiny is not a straight line.

Here are three false beliefs of the mind:

1. The mind wants you to believe that security and stability are most important.

While security and stability are important, seeking them above all else is not realistic. Seeking only security can lead to panic, fear, and entropy. Those who are constantly seeking security never seem to find it. I coach many women who are seeking love. They want a stable relationship with a husband and marriage that will provide them security in the long-term. While most of us want love and security, there are no guarantees in life. We can strive for a long-term, stable relationship, but life is too unpredictable. Furthermore, relationships take work and dedication on both sides. In my coaching practice, I find that the women who are the most desperate to find security and stability end up chasing men away or settle for men who are deeply insecure.

The same thing happens when you search for security in a job or career. When that is your focal point, chances are you'll remain in a job that is not satisfying.

The mind's need for security is the opposite of faith. Faith requires you to believe that your higher power is working to help you succeed in all walks of life. A sense of faith says that you're not alone in this great big universe.

2. The mind wants you to believe that things stay the same; when in reality, things are in constant motion.

We are all aware of the trap that many married couples fall into after 5, 10, or 15 years of marriage. They get frustrated when they see that the person they married is not the same as they are in the present moment. You may even hear yourself or others say to their spouse, "You're not the person I married. Who are you?" That is a very good question. We are all in a state of constant change and it's a good thing too. Can you imagine what you would be like if you weren't continually learning and growing? And that is the reason why so many love relationships tend to change status. Younger people who get married may go through more change. Older people getting married may have a better handle on what they want and who they are as individuals. But in either case, recalibration in relationships is a constant.

The same lesson applies to all aspects of life. The mind and the ego will tell you that things must stay the same to be comfortable and predictable. But if you look back on your life, you will notice that the best things happened when big changes occurred. And much of the time, those big changes or periods of growth will seem to have occurred when you were experiencing some type of pain or discomfort.

Let's get real here. If you never experience pain or discomfort, then what is the motivation for change? I know there have been periods in my life where things were just okay. I went about my daily life and routine because nothing was really wrong. But it's when I started to get antsy or uncomfortable that I started exploring ways in which I could change something to feel better. Sometimes the solution was as simple as getting out of daily routine and taking a vacation. Other times this discomfort required a huge change like moving into a new home or losing some weight, for example.

3. The mind will tell you that if you don't live up to society's standards and expectations, then you're not worthy.
Much pain comes from the fact that societal standards have led us to believe that we must conform to what society expects of us

versus what we expect of ourselves. Society says that you must graduate from secondary school, go to a college or university, graduate, get a job, get married, buy a home, have some kids, and give back to society in some way. Again it goes back to that linear thinking of *how life works*. The problem is, not everyone is hard-wired to perform in such a linear fashion. Talents come in all shapes and sizes. Growth patterns change depending on previous life experiences as well as your inborn personality traits. Many people suffer because they compare themselves to society's expectations. When they see that they're not living up to those expectations, they give up or turn to things like drugs and alcohol to ease the pain of not fitting in.

The truth is, no one can tell you what the trajectory of your life should look like. I once met a woman who raised her kids, had a whole other career, and then decided to put herself through medical school at age fifty. She is now an emergency-room physician at age sixty-five. I've also read stories about seventy-year-olds who go to college for the first time and finish with a degree.

Your life path and purpose will change as you evolve and grow. When you live from your spiritual self and are in constant contact with your higher power, you're better able to measure your life by a different standard.

I often get asked, "How do I know my life purpose?" I have done workshops on this topic and it's something I address in *The Wheel of Healing with Ayurveda* in the chapter on *dharma*. But with my life experience I can say this; you don't have a singular life purpose. Your life path may have a common theme. But the work you do with it will change and evolve over time. For example, I always knew I would be a speaker in front of large audiences. When I was a child, I was involved in acting and the theatre. Therefore, I thought I would grow up to be an actress. What I didn't know then was that I would speak in front of audiences on a social media platform called YouTube. I couldn't have known because the platform didn't yet exist when I was a child.

If you are always measuring your life with the lives of others around you, you will suffer. You will also have pain if you're trying to live up to someone else's standards that they've set up for your life. Furthermore, you will suffer if you aren't able to see your part in the bigger picture, meaning, your contributions to the world however small they may seem.

THE SOUL'S CALLING

Have you ever come to a place in life where you were going about your business doing the normal things you do in life when, BAM, you came to a sudden realization? That realization might have been, *OMG I hate where I live.* Or *I don't want to be married to my spouse anymore.* Or *I hate my job.* It's a time in your life when these epiphanies seem to be coming out of nowhere. You were happy doing what you were doing. In the very least you were okay with it. But these realizations hit you like a bolt of lightening and then there was no turning back. Some people might refer to them as a mid-life crisis even if they happen in your 20s or 30s. I happen to call them your soul's calling.

These realizations have happened to me many times in the course of my lifetime. Often I would question or blame myself for them. I would say things like, *What's wrong with you? You're very blessed Michelle. Why are you so unhappy with this now?* As I reflect back on those moments, I now realize that if they had not happened in that way, I wouldn't be where I am today. Those sudden jolts were messages from my soul that the lessons, in that time period, were done and that it was time to move onto something else.

The flow of the universe operates as an ebb and flow. When you flow with it, occurrences will come about to make you move in a different direction. If you choose to flow against it, you will reach obstacle after obstacle and much pain will result.

A baby in its mother's womb is warm, fed, and perfectly cared for. But after nine months or so the baby becomes too big for its uterine habitat. Inside at 40-weeks gestation, the baby has restricted space. It must leave its comfortable but snug environment for a new one. If it protested its birth, the baby would die as the placenta would wear out, deteriorate, and fail to provide nourishment.

Your soul knows when it's time to leave, grow, or move on. When that time comes, you will feel uncomfortable. You will have a nagging feeling that something is not quite right. That unsettled feeling will continue to grow until you start to make the changes you know you must make. Instead of chastising yourself like I have done (and perhaps you have done in the past), celebrate for passing the tests of life. *Yay! It's time to graduate and move on to the next level.*

Like a high school senior with *senioritis*, this awakening or epiphany accompanied by your soul's tugging gives you a sense of urgency. You feel like you must move on. But just as that senior in high school must finish his semester and take his final exams, so must you. As you move forward toward your soul's next calling, take the time to carefully tie up any loose ends so that you don't have to go back and rework the lessons you've already completed.

Your soul's calling is unique to you. Just as no two snowflakes are alike, nor are two sets of fingerprints; your soul's code is completely unique. That is the reason why it's impossible for any other human being to tell you what you should be doing or how you should be living your life. We often get stuck when we have to rectify what we hear through our inner voice with what the outer world says we should or shouldn't do.

Assuming that you are of sound mind, without the influence of drugs or alcohol and without the negative effects of an untreated mental illness or brain disease, the truth of your heart's desires in conjunction with your soul's calling must supersede all opinions of others. The main reason why much suffering exists is because societies have been formed to help people fit into a mold. Well, what happens when you don't fit into any of those molds? You are left feeling inadequate and less than capable of living a successful and happy life.

Because I was pushed and prodded to move away from my soul's purpose for the entirety of my childhood, I was confused once I reached adulthood. As a result, I changed my major in college five or six times and it took me six years to get a bachelor's degree. And even then, I didn't graduate with the degree I wanted because I had a child while still attending college. I was lost and a mess.

In the end I'm grateful to have been a parent early on in life. Yet through my experience of being told, on a constant basis, what I must do with my life, I vowed to never tell my kids what they must do in the way of studies or a career. I always encouraged them to find their own path. I once heard the following bit of advice. I'm not sure of the source, but I believe it was Dr. Wayne Dyer who taught it in one of his speeches. The advice goes, "Who must you wake up to every single day for your entire life? And who must you go to bed with every single day for your entire life? The answer is, *you.*" You are the only person you *have* to live with your entire life. Therefore, if you can't live with you because you haven't listened to your inner voice or your soul's calling, you've got a big problem. And that problem is usually laced with a lot of suffering.

But let's get back to the basics. You might now be wondering what you can do to overcome societal standards and connect with your higher power and your higher self. In the next chapter we'll explore your spiritual awakening to be able to overcome limitations and live from a higher state of consciousness.

CHAPTER THREE: RECAP OF LESSONS LEARNED

1. Connecting to your higher self and your higher power is the first step away from the ego.
2. Direct experience creates your relationship with God.
3. Finding out who or what you are living for can give you a clear vision on your life path and purpose.
4. The integration into wholeness happens when you understand your place in the universe.
5. The measure by which you live your life must come from your inner knowing and not by someone else's standards or wishes for you.
6. Your soul's calling might cause you to make big changes in your life at various points throughout your life.

FOUR

AWAKENING TO YOUR SPIRITUAL SELF

Spirituality is not some external goal that one must seek, but a part of the divine core of each of us, which we must reveal. —B.K.S. Iyengar, Light on Life

You have, without a doubt, taken a glimpse into your spiritual self. Your soul is your truest identity as it's ageless, timeless, and spaceless. It existed before you were born and it will be with you after you die. When we introduce the concept of transcending suffering, we must become aware of our soul and how to access it at any given moment.

That is why the practices of silence and meditation are essential. With all of the noise of the mind and daily life, it can become nearly impossible to distinguish between the voices of the ego and that of your higher spiritual self. The more you access silence, the more you'll be able to experience your awakened spiritual self.

THE ORCHESTRATOR OF EVENTS

When I was 8 or 9-years-old, I would have this conversation with myself every morning, *I wonder if I'm going to have a good day or bad day*. I would then go over the events of the previous day to determine if they were good or bad. Then I would scan over the day to come and see if that meant my day would be a good one or not. I did this every single day for years. In previous chapters, I explained that I grew up in a home filled with turmoil. My mother was angry most of the time. I always felt like I was doing something wrong, when in reality I was doing nothing wrong most of the time. It wasn't until I became a teenager that I threw in the towel. I reasoned, *Well, if she's always accusing me of doing something wrong, I'll rebel and really do something wrong*. I believe the reason behind my morning conversation with myself had to do with the fact that I felt completely out of control when it came to my own life. I became terrified most of the time that I might have a bad day.

Now you may or may not have grown up in a dysfunctional household. But what I do know about human behavior is that you might still feel out of control when it comes to your life. For me, it was about being controlled by other authoritative adults. For you, it could be about the fear of losing a job or a spouse. You might have insecurities and fears that you adopted in childhood for various reasons.

Here is the truth; you have more control over your destiny and the outcome of your life than you think. You have even more control over your thoughts, feelings, and reactions. Control over your own life comes from the inside rather than the outside.

Right now you may be wondering, *How is that so? I don't feel in control. I feel like everything and everyone around me determines my happiness or wellbeing.* I know it feels that way right now. It's time to begin changing that perspective.

WITNESSING AWARENESS

The change in perspective is called *witnessing awareness.* You can call it by many other names but the purpose is the same. The idea is to shift awareness from your body, mind, intellect, and ego toward your spirit. In all things you will be *standing* in your spiritual self, *watching* the other aspects of yourself. Shifting to this perspective gives you the space and time to see everything from a broader view. When you're caught up in life, it can feel like you're a piece of driftwood being tossed about on turbulent waters. In this state, you're stuck in action and reaction mode. From this perspective, you feel out of control. But when you step back into your spiritual self, you start to pause and think things through before acting and reacting.

Much of our actions and reactions are a result of conditioning. And that is why we don't feel free. In becoming the witness or the observer you are able to see a whole host of new choices. Instead of limitations, you begin to see possibilities.

Let me give you an example that affected the entire world in 2020. The outbreak of the Coronavirus or COVID-19 pandemic was the cause for panic worldwide. Because the Western model has limited beliefs on how to contain and treat disease, advice has been limited to increasing sanitary conditions, social distancing, and long-term quarantine. Fear created widespread alarm over the fact that modern science would take a long time to create a vaccine. As an Ayurvedic practitioner I know that Eastern medical practices has many additional ways of preventing a viral infection. Since most alternative healthcare practices are continually rebuked by modern science, these effective solutions aren't in the mainstream. One method is to keep viruses and bacteria from growing in the oral and nasal cavities. The best way to do this is to insert natural oils that are viral static such as pure organic sesame oil or coconut oil or ghee. All you need to do is apply these oils inside the nostrils 3-4 times a day and gargle with them to coat the mouth and throat. These oils will prevent viruses from growing. Additionally, panic over depleted supplies of hand sanitizer and facemasks caused hoarding. Again, herbal medicine has remedies to keep your hands and body naturally bacteria and virus free. You can add a few drops of lavender essential oil to your hand soap for example. You can take herbs to boost your immune system. In fact, there are thousands of ways you can keep yourself healthy in the midst of a worldwide viral outbreak. The modern world has a limited view. So instead of people operating from their spiritual selves with an enhanced and broadened view with creative solutions, they've acted and reacted with fear and terror (ego traits of survival). Operating from your spiritual self you might reason, *Millions of people have been affected by disease and pandemics throughout centuries. Before modern medicine we did have solutions. What were those solutions? And how did people find and use them? What does the Earth give us naturally that we're not using?*

When we're caught up in the problem and are in the trenches, so to speak, it can become extremely difficult to see outside of any problem in life. Yet as we shift perspective to becoming the witness of these events including our actions and reactions to them, creative solutions seem to come out of nowhere.

Most often we tend to see solutions to obstacles in terms of polar opposites. Things are either black or white, yes or no, with little wiggle room for something in between. Going back to the example of the 2020 Coronavirus pandemic, I was talking with my with a friend the other day and explained, "The way modern medicine has always worked, for the past 250 years, is like they have a hammer and they are looking for one nail." In other words, if you are only looking for a nail to fit your hammer, you are limited in your choices. In the case of the pandemic, large health organizations have said that humans cannot return to normal life until a vaccine is created, tested, and able to be used on everyone. This is the prime example of one hammer and one nail. But what if each country gave incentives to scientists and proposed a think tank of many creative ideas to combat the spread of a virus? Imagine the possibilities that could come out such a think tank. You can have many different solutions toward either finding a cure or an alternative solution to stop the spread of a threatening virus. Furthermore, coming up with many creative solutions would help in the event of a different disease outbreak. Having a singular solution for a specific problem only limits that solution to the one specific event, in this case the 2020 Coronavirus or Covid-19 virus.

As you move into a state of witnessing awareness, you begin to defy physical limitations including that which confines us to logic. You begin to allow the intelligence of the entire universe to infiltrate your mind. And this can only be done as you get quiet and allow the mind, intellect, and ego to subside, while your spiritual self takes the leading role in your life.

BECOMING THE OBSERVER

As you sit in silence and let your spiritual self come into the light, you begin to observe yourself and your life differently. Additionally, you start to observe others and the world in a detached way. You notice more. In the quiet waters of your mind, you're able to discern better.

Prior to becoming aware, your mind was too crazy with thoughts to be able to see clearly. It is very difficult, in the turbulent mind, to have proper discernment. Your vision is too clouded to be able to observe much of anything. Most often you are too busy catering to your ego or mind. Otherwise, you're giving in to what others desire for you or striving to fit into society's demands. In the stillness of your own silence you have lifted the veil of your own perception.

When it comes to your own behavior, you might now observe, *I don't really like it when I do this or say that to someone. I wonder why I acted that way all of those years.* It can be shocking to hear and see yourself as you observe because you may have never taken a look at your previous behavior. The beauty in being the observer is not to judge, but to have an expanded number of choices as to how to act and react in the future.

Then when it comes to others, you're able to notice when they are acting from the ego, mind, or intellect and have more compassion for them. Through your newfound experience as the observer, you start to realize that action and reaction through the lens of the ego, mind, and intellect kept you imprisoned.

Oftentimes, living from the perspective of the subtle body keeps you in victim mode, survival mode, or in a constant state of arguments with others to prove that you're right. You find very little tranquility in the perspective of the subtle body. Most sadness, frustration, and helplessness come from these states of being.

Yet observation mode starts to offer you choices you never thought you had. It offers you freedom and joy.

Let me give you an example. If you have a long commute to work you may have the mindset that it's an annoyance. During the commute, you may grumble that other drivers are impolite, aggressive, and that the city you live in is constantly congested with motor vehicles. You may even get stressed at the thought of your morning or evening commute as you anticipate the struggles that lie ahead. I live in Los Angeles, and until I moved here I thought I had experienced heavy traffic. Los Angeles redefines the word "traffic." It can be nearly impossible to find a time in the day where the highways are not congested.

But I divert. Let's go back to the example. Imagine the turmoil of operating from the mind, intellect and ego. From that viewpoint, you might have conversations with yourself like, *Mondays are the worst. I wish more people would get off the road.* Or, *There better not be an accident or I'm doomed.* Then when you're on the road your inner dialogue may change to, *Hey jerk, move over and don't come into my lane.* Or, *Speed up and get out of my way.* Or, *Stop driving like an old lady, don't you know you're slowing down traffic?*

But when you shift gears and go into observation mode, your experience becomes much more pleasant. I used to be a stressed out driver. Then in 2018, I started to work at Disneyland in Anaheim, California. I live near Los Angeles, so I had a 45-minute commute on good days. In order to make my life easier I had to shift perspective about my commute to it being a pleasant experience. As a result I would treat myself to a Starbucks on my way to work a few times per week. I would listen to books on MP3s and take motivational courses on CD. On the way home I would use my commute as an opportunity to catch up with family and friends on the East Coast. All in all I felt that I used that time efficiently and the experience brought me joy.

Certainly there are people, many people, who still consider a commute to be a hindrance to their quality of life. And they suffer because of it. Much of that suffering comes because they don't believe they have a choice. If they were to observe the bigger picture, they would be able to see that they always have a choice. That choice might come down to, *If you can't change your circumstances, you can certainly change your reaction to them.*

LETTING GO OF SOCIAL CONDITIONING

One of the greatest sources of suffering when living from the ego, mind, and intellect is trying to adhere to the rules of social conditioning. As you move toward living from the perspective of your spiritual self, much of this type of suffering goes away. Of course, everyone has the need to fit in on some level. By truly living from your spiritual self, you shouldn't have to be a social outcast. But you won't feel inclined to bend over backwards to adhere to rules and social norms that don't make sense for you.

I have many clients who are miserable because they are trying to live up to the expectations of their parents, culture, religion, friends, and society in general. Oftentimes, they are frozen from moving forward in their own lives for fear of what others might think. They are caught in the trap of loved ones who try and control their lives. As a result they fear the consequences of stepping out and doing their own thing. It truly is a tragedy when the people we love and care about feel the need to control our lives and choices.

Living from your spiritual self takes bravery and a warrior spirit. Not everyone is going to agree that the global picture gives you more choices. You may even be shunned by the people closest to you. But living from your truest and highest self is one of the only ways you can transcend suffering. In reality, no one knows your life path but you. No person can pretend to know the calling of your heart. Humans who have accomplished the most in the way of inventions or even social movements dropped the confines of social conditioning like a hot potato.

One of my favorite role models, Julia Child, was told that she couldn't attend the Cordon Bleu cooking school in Paris because she was a woman and an American. Yet in 1951, Julia Child was the first woman to graduate from the Cordon Bleu at age thirty-nine.

Mahatma Gandhi, a brown Indian man and a lawyer with a first class ticket in South Africa was not allowed to sit in first class. That denial from society was the catalyst that began India's liberation from the British Empire. Steve Jobs dropped out of college and began Apple computers in his garage. Nelson Mandela fought to end Apartheid in South Africa from a prison. Walt Disney, a man with no money or education but a dream, started Disney Studios in Hollywood with just a few dollars left from selling a camera to take a train to California. The examples are endless. If you want to know what it is truly like to transcend suffering and let your spirit soar, kick the confines of social conditioning.

DAILY PRACTICE TO RENEW YOUR CONNECTION

Living from the point of view of the mind, intellect, and ego is the norm. You might be inclined to think that you'll have an "aha!" moment and in an instant you'll be living from your spiritual self. I would love to be the one who tells you that's true. However, living in society *and* living from your spiritual self are a constant challenge. With practice it gets easier over time. But don't think for a moment that you can just meditate for a year straight and say joyfully, "I'm cured now!" The most dedicated and enlightened spiritual masters meditate and pray daily. You must get in touch with your spiritual self every single day if you want to maintain the joys of its presence in your life.

I learned how to meditate in November 2007. When I learned, my intention was not to learn to meditate. I wanted to complete a certification to be able to teach others about Ayurveda. Knowing the mental and spiritual rigor it would take to teach others about this ancient healing system, The Chopra Center co-founders, Dr. Deepak Chopra and Dr. David Simon knew that every one of their teachers must be meditating daily. Whenever I tell the story about learning to meditate I jokingly say, "I went to that meditation retreat kicking and screaming." While that isn't entirely true, I wasn't happy about it until I learned and experienced my first week of meditation. It's not until you're meditating regularly that you realize how crazy your mind is. Now thirteen years later I can tell you that meditation is the most valuable tool I have, hands down. Meditation made me a much nicer person, a more compassionate person, and made me much calmer in general. It did the work of getting me connected to my higher self. Yet thirteen years later I can also tell you that I meditate daily or nearly every day and have done so the entire time. Without my meditation practice I wouldn't be able to be the teacher I am today. It's by seeing the bigger picture daily that I'm able to help my students see solutions to their problems.

In addition to meditation I have a practice of prayer and gratitude. Surrendering to God and being grateful daily are two practices I could not do without. Here's the reason. The ego wants to tell you that *you* are the center of the universe. Furthermore, the ego will say things like, *You don't need God. That's for weak peo-*

ple. *You've got you. Isn't that all you need? You're a good person.* Here's what I've learned from life experience. As soon as you say things like, "I've got me. I'm a good person." It puts you at the center of the universe. And guess what? When you're the center, anything goes. You can try to be a "good person." But then you have nothing to measure that against. If you are the measuring stick, then when you slip up, no problem, just lower your morals or standards. Plus, it's a lot of pressure to be the center of the universe. Generally speaking, in my experience, those who say they are atheists are the most cynical, jaded, and unhappy people in the world. Here is the reason. If you are the center of your universe and if you can't control anyone or anything (because let's face it, you're not a deity), you become bitter. That bitterness comes from everyone else not acting according to what you think should happen. It also puts a lot of weight on your shoulders. As your own universe and your own "god," if something goes wrong in your life, then it's all your fault. There is no bigger picture. If you are an atheist, I have nothing against you. My observations noted above are what I've seen time and again in different atheist humans who have crossed my path.

When I know there is a power greater than myself, it causes me to be humble and show humility toward others. In this humility I know that I didn't plan the whole universe, so I don't know why things happen and what the outcomes must be. In addition, surrendering to my higher power makes me a nicer person because I'm not trying to run your life either. I know that you have your path and I have mine. Our paths may cross but when it's time, our paths might also diverge. Surrendering to my higher power also makes me more compassionate. As I submit to God and get on my knees, I tend to judge you less. While I might not understand why certain people do misguided or bad things, I can have humility that God is guiding their way. By surrendering to my higher power I also have respect for all living things. If God is the one who created me, he also created everything that lives. Are you starting to see now that continuous spiritual practices will take you out of your ego and move you daily toward your higher spiritual self?

THE BASICS OF MEDITATION

In many of my books I've written extensively about meditation. My book *Chakra Healing for Vibrant Energy* includes seven guided meditations. In addition, my book on integrative health, *Enlightened Medicine Your Power to Get Well Now,* has an in depth explanation with cited studies on the health benefits of meditation. While I don't necessarily recommend learning meditation from a book, you can certainly gain pointers on the basics of it.

Meditation takes you beyond the mind, intellect, and ego (the subtle body) and into the causal body, which, if you remember, includes your personal soul, the collective soul, and the universal soul. The chatter of the mind can be disturbing. If you are able to lower the number of thoughts, you can settle down into your spiritual self. When I teach my meditation course, I explain that as you sit down to meditate, it feels like you're floating on the surface of the ocean with turbulent waters. But as you continue, it's like diving down into deeper waters where it's much calmer. Additionally, I recommend the use of a mantra to help you get deeper into your meditation practice. The word *mantra* comes from two Sanskrit words, *man,* which means "mind" and *tra,* which means "instrument." Thus, the mantra is an instrument of the mind designed to hold it in place while you, the spirit, sinks into peace. Your mind and its chatter are natural. The mind's job is to think thoughts. The more you fight it, the more difficult it will be to meditate. However, if you sit down to meditate and repeat your mantra, you're not in a constant battle with your mind but simply changing your focus. During your meditation practice, your mind will wander and try to get your attention. As long as you bring your focus back to your mantra, the mind will eventually give up. When this happens, you move from ego to spirit and begin to experience the blessings of the soul. In the meditation practice I teach, we call this "slipping into the gap." What this means is that you move beyond space, time, and causality and enter into the silent space between your thoughts. In this space you access your soul. You gain greater awareness of the bigger picture and the qualities of spirit. These qualities are what we all crave. Some of these qualities include: unconditional love, joy, serenity, freedom, perfect health, compassion, empathy, abundance, and creativity.

The goal of meditation is not to try and reach the gap. Nor is it to quickly grab a few qualities of spirit and take them with you like a fast food carryout. The goal of meditation is to meditate. Do your meditation practice; hopefully twice per day, and trust in the wisdom that created you that your practice will work.

In the Western world, we are accustomed to being extremely goal-oriented. Believe me, I am not spared of this mentality any-more than you are. I have been an over-achiever my entire life. However, throughout the years, I've learned to not be goal-oriented when it comes to meditation.

In the past twelve years, hundreds of my students initially struggled with the notion that learning and practicing meditation cannot be put into a well-defined box with a definite goal and finish date. After the first lesson, students come back to me with the complaint, *I've been trying to meditate but A, B, or C problem comes in the way and I find I'm not very good at it.* If you were learning to ride a bike or drive a car, I could see that you might have a real-life measuring stick to assess your progress. But meditation doesn't work like that. If you are spending ten minutes a day meditating, then you're doing it. If you're sitting in meditation but thinking thousands of thoughts, you're still meditating. And if you happen to meditate and fall asleep then, guess what? You're still meditating.

A meditation practice is not a sprint, but a long, long, *long,* marathon. The more you practice, the more you will see the results in your daily life. Furthermore, the more you *try* to meditate, the more frustrated you will become. Meditation is a practice in surrender. You must surrender to your body, to your breath, and to the world around you. Just as prayer and gratitude bring you humility, so does meditation.

While guided meditations are certainly helpful and a great way to start, I would highly recommend seeking out a well-established meditation teacher to introduce you to this skill. The most profound meditation practices are done in silence with a mantra. I have taught the Chopra Center Primordial Sound Meditation Course since 2009 and it's been the most beneficial practice I have found.

YOU WERE NEVER BORN, THEREFORE, YOU CAN NEVER DIE

The most valuable lesson I learned, first from Dr. Wayne Dyer, was, "You were never born, therefore, you can never die." The realization of this concept was the most liberating of my life.

Your spiritual self, in other words, your soul, is boundless, spaceless, and timeless. Your soul is eternal. It has always existed and will always exist. It has no beginning in time and no ending in time so where could it go? Your soul agreed to travel into this lifetime, take on a human incarnation for about a hundred years or less, and then go back to being a soul with no body, perhaps. If you believe in re-incarnation then you will probably move into another human form and recommence the journey as you learn more lessons. When you truly realize this, do you see the liberation in it? In this knowing, you will never fear death. Because what is death for a soul? It's just a new life or a new phase in the journey.

Ever since I was about 10-years-old, I never really feared death. Before that I was terrified of death. I would pray daily, *God give me life with perfect health for 100 years.* But after that I just didn't freak out about it. The concept of death didn't bother me for my-self or others. (When I had kids it was a whole other story, but I diverge.) I remember my mom getting freaked out about death constantly. In the face of her worry, I took a nonchalant approach, "If it happens, it happens." She often told me I was cold or callous for saying so. I answered that she lacked faith. My mother is very pious and I grew up religiously. But even as a kid I thought, *Well, if you die, you're with God, so it can't be that bad. I don't know what all the fuss is about. You're going to a better place.* Yet my mom sent conflicting messages. On one hand, she was saying to trust in God and that when we die we go to heaven. But on the other hand she was obsessed with death like it was nobody's business. She would say things like, "Go visit your grandparents, you don't know how long they're going to be around." And if she got a migraine, she would talk about her impending funeral. It was insane.

My take on the matter is, you either believe in a higher power and that where you're headed next is good or you don't believe, and when you die, you're dirt. There really is no in-between.

Yet the knowledge that you are not your body, mind, or intellect and that who you are is eternal, is freeing on every level. It doesn't mean that you won't have respect for this human life you chose. In fact, knowing that your soul chose this life gives you even more respect for it. Here is my philosophy on the subject: *If I learn my lessons well and don't create any negative karma, then the next time around I get to live a more awesome life.*

Much suffering is created by the fear of death. Some people try to live a "safe life" and play it small so that they don't take too many risks. But as a result they're miserable because they're not living the life they truly desire. Others mask the fear of death with substances, because they can't bear to think that they aren't where they should be in life. Yet when you release worry about the amount of time you have left and focus on the quality of the time you do have, you tend to not live at such tragic extremes.

Throughout this chapter I've talked about connecting with your spiritual self and moving toward witnessing awareness, but until you experience it firsthand, it seems surreal. Start infusing spiritual practices into your daily life and you'll begin to see the fruits of your labor in a great way.

CHAPTER FOUR: RECAP OF LESSONS LEARNED

1. Silence and meditation are essential for connecting to your higher spiritual self.

2. Control over your own life comes from the inside.

3. Witnessing awareness is shifting your awareness from your mind, ego, and intellect to your individual soul.

4. Connecting with your higher power daily through gratitude and prayer helps you get out of your ego.

5. Spiritual practices are a lifelong commitment to combat the pull back into the mind, intellect, and ego.

FIVE

THE PAST IS YOUR TEACHER, NOT YOUR TETHER

Forget the past. The vanished lives of all men are dark with many shames. Human conduct is ever unreliable until man is anchored in the Divine. –Parmahansa Yogananda

For better or for worse, most people stay tethered to their past. In fact, attachment to the past is one of the greatest sources of suffering. The problem with the past is that it's, well, in the past. You can't alter or modify it. It's just there. And staying attached to it is just as silly as chaining yourself to a bedpost with a five-foot chain that barely reaches the door. You try to step forward and move out, but each time you're tugged back to the bedpost. But guess what? You're the one who chained yourself there in the first place. You're the one choosing to stay tethered to your past. No one is forcing you to do it.

The past is designed to teach you something. Most of the time we don't ask for the lessons that life gives us, but they show up nonetheless. And if you look to the past as serving you a delicious dish of lessons, you won't tend to get so caught up in the "why" of it all. Additionally, you won't become attached to the meaning of the past as if it were there to intentionally punish you.

I did not have a rosy past. My past is riddled with terribly misguided people and loads of unfairness. For many years of my early adulthood, I was angry. I was angry that the people who are supposed to love you could mistreat you. I was angry that controlling people told me what I could and couldn't do with my studies and career. Then one day I decided to stop the madness. Through a lot of soul-searching, I found that I could control my own destiny regardless of my past. I made the decision that if things happened to me, there were reasons, even if I couldn't understand them. As a result, I stopped being angry and wallowing in self-pity. Some days I truly don't get why certain things had to happen, but I'm content in knowing that those events were a part of God's plan.

WHAT TIME ZONE ARE YOU LIVING IN?

Throughout my life I've always had an interest in meeting new people. I'm always fascinated in hearing people's stories, such as where they come from, the way they grew up, and the things that make up their family culture. The interesting piece about meeting a lot of people and hearing their stories is that you can get a keen sense on the time zone they're living in. When I refer to time zone in this section, I'm talking about the past, present, or future.

Most people are either living in the past or the future. As a grand assessment, those who are living in the past are usually the unhappiest. Those who live in the future, might be happy, but seem to be struggling in the present. And those who live in the present are usually the happiest of them all.

Heal Yourself: A Return to Wholeness

Staying rooted in any one of the three, however, can be danger-ous and cause suffering. For example, yogic philosophy says, "You must attain present moment awareness to reduce suffering." While this statement is true, have you ever known anyone who was so rooted in present moment awareness that they didn't see the need to work or make money? I have certainly seen these people. You can have a *hakuna matata* attitude, but somewhere down the line someone needs to pay the rent or electric bill. Then there are those who live mostly for the future. They are constantly chasing goals and deadlines. It seems that they cannot stop for a minute to smell the roses or even take a breath.

The healthiest time zone *is* living in the now, but with an appre-ciation for your past and a clear vision of your future. Two of the most prominent mental illnesses today, anxiety and depression, are diseases of staying stuck in the two other time zones. Think about it. Depression is a mental disease that keeps you stuck in the past. And any anxiety disorder keeps you in a state of projection on an imaginary or potential future.

Most people are depressed because of what happened to them. They are stuck in how they were treated as a child, teenager, or young adult. Or they're stuck in how an ex-spouse or ex-lover treat-ed them. Depressed people are also fixated on details of events of the past and relive them over and over in their mind. They're caught in a web of wishing how things could have been different "if only." Their mantras are for example:

If only I had said this or done this.
If only my mother would have treated me better.
If only my spouse wouldn't have cheated on me.
If only I hadn't been bullied as a child.

If only I had graduated from college, I wouldn't have these financial troubles today.

Those who suffer from anxiety disorders have a whole different conversation going on. They are stuck in future casting. They live in constant fear of what might come about. Their mantra phrase is, "what if." Their mantras are for example:

What if I don't have enough money to pay my bills.
What if I lose my job? I'll be out on the streets.
What if my spouse leaves me?
What if I get cancer?
What if my children get hit by a car?

And the worry about a potential future that may or may not happen goes on. Well, what happens if you have both of these disorders. Can you imagine living in the past *and* living in an imaginary future at the same time while skipping over the present? That is the cause for a lot of suffering. A person who lives in both the past and future within the confines of anxiety and depression might say things like:

My last two boyfriends cheated on me. I'm pretty sure that my future ones will too. If that happens. I'm doomed.
I lost my job when the economy took a downturn. What if I lose my job again when the economy gets tough again?
I got cancer once. What if I get it again. I probably will. I'm more susceptible now.

Heal Yourself: A Return to Wholeness

The spinning cycle of going from past to future and future to past keeps you in a loop of doom and gloom. Why? Because you're skipping over the present. You're failing to observe what's happening in the here and now.

After my diagnosis and treatments for thyroid cancer, I was on the wrong dosage and medication for my body. The result was that I experienced a lot of anxiety and depression. I was 28-years-old and hadn't experienced either prior to the cancer treatment. Sure, I had experienced the natural ups and downs of life, but this was more clinical. Inside my mind I *knew* it was a result of not being on the correct medication. But I couldn't find doctors who believed me. They said that my numbers looked fine and that my body should be adapting well. And yet it wasn't. For the first time in my life I was having panic attacks. I was so depressed sometimes that I couldn't move. The worst part of it was, the more I tried to convince doctors that "this isn't me" the more they told me that I was crazy. One even told me to go see a psychiatrist to get on anti-anxiety medications. So I did. I got a prescription for Xanax. When I felt a panic attack coming on, I would take it. But it didn't really help. It would just make me drowsy. At that time, in the year 2000, the Internet was in its infancy. Yet I was able to find a series of cassette tapes made by a woman who had suffered anxiety and panic attacks her whole adult life. In fact, she was so crippled by them that she didn't leave her home for eight years. How did she overcome them? By living in the present moment. She told the story of how she began to observe her present life. She started to appreciate the things around her and notice that life wasn't so scary after all. From what I remember, she started with small things like the bushes outside of her house or the color and smell of the grass. She began noticing the perfection of nature and how it's not worried at all. In her tapes, I remember hearing a story about her making it all the way to the grocery store. When she got to the frozen food section, she started laughing out loud. She explained that it gave her so much joy just to be standing in the frozen food section and be completely fine. The lesson to her was that real life is not scary at all. Your past is not scary because it's not here now. And your future is not scary because you have no idea what will happen. You can only live in the present moment. And if your present moment is *scary*, do what you can to change it. The only really scary things are the stories in your mind.

As for my story, I remember the day when I started to over-come the anxiety and depression. It didn't happen all at once, but it was a stepping-stone. It was late February. I was living in Northern Virginia and I went outside to get some fresh air. To the right side of me, I noticed that daffodils, or the first spring flowers of that region, had sprung up. Seeing those beautiful yellow flowers made me so happy. At that moment, I was filled with joy. Suddenly, I knew that I wasn't depressed or anxious and I *knew* that I wasn't crazy. I got up at once, ran to my room, took the prescription of Xanax, and sprinted out to the dumpster. I threw it in and came back with new resolve to find the solution to my medical problem. My solution came from noticing the present moment.

The present moment is your anchor. You can float backward toward your past or drift into your future, but stay anchored in the present. Notice the things around you. Be grateful for the little things and big things. If you can't find something to be grateful for in your present moment, you haven't looked hard enough. For example, when I see someone in a wheelchair I say to God, "Thank

you for my legs and thank you that they are strong and healthy."
If all else fails say, "Thank you for the air I have to breathe." Then
observe your breath, each breath, and it will help you stay rooted
in the present moment.

THE PAST AS YOUR STORY

When you live in the past you become attached to your story. Your
story then becomes your calling card. We've already established
that you are constantly changing and growing so what was true
yesterday might not be true today.

It's easy to get caught up in your story. You might say things
like:

I'm a cancer survivor.

I'm an addict.

I'm a diabetic.

I was abused.

I'm divorced.

My parents mistreated me.

I'm disabled.

I come from a poor home.

Your story doesn't define who you are now. Even a line from your
story only defines a singular portion of the entirety of your life.
You may be a cancer survivor, for example, but is that who you *really* are? Earlier in the book I talked about my friend's mother who
survived a deadly form of ovarian cancer twice. After overcoming
the odds, not one but two times, she was asked by several cancer
support groups to come and speak about her story. Immediately
she refused, not because she was callous and uncaring, but because she didn't want to have to relive that story time and again.
Additionally, she didn't want to define herself by that story.

When you relive your past through your story, you are in a constant state of reliving that pain. Dr. Wayne Dyer used to say (and I'm paraphrasing), "People walk around with their past, dragging it around like it's a big bag of manure. They carry it around all day and sometimes stop, put the bag down, open it, and smear it all over themselves. Then the wonder why their life smells so bad." Using your past to help others in controlled situations, such as telling your story at an Alcoholics Anonymous meeting is fine. But making your story your calling card isn't healthy.

The question you must ask yourself is, *Why do I insist upon making the story of my past a repetitious affair? In what way does it serve me?* In my experience through coaching and mentoring others, many people want to keep those stories alive because it keeps them in victim mode. They're looking for others to feel sorry for them or give them special treatment. Other people use those stories as an excuse to not move forward. And yet for others, they tell those stories to try and make them look better when they aren't willing to do more to make their present situation move forward.

To illustrate the last example, think about a person you've met who has bragged about one great accomplishment from their past. Are they riding on that accomplishment even if it was 10, 15, or 20 years ago? Here's an example of what that story might sound like: *When I was 21-years-old I was in a band that got signed to a record label. We opened for the (insert popular rock band here) one time. It was great man!* Then when you ask them what they've done with music since then, they usually go on with excuses of all the misfortunes of their life that has prevented them from ever making music again. Even though that story sounds like a good one, the pain is the same. That person living in the past with that story is refusing to move forward and create a new one.

The way you can change that is by saying, "My story is what I'm doing today." For example, for me today I'm a mom, friend, and daughter. I write books, produce YouTube videos, do yoga, run, and meditate daily. I love to eat Indian food. I'm very obsessive about my health. And I like to smile and laugh a lot. Tomorrow may be different. But that's who I am today. In addition, that story doesn't fully include everything that I am today. It's just a little peek into my life. Interestingly enough, if I were to ask a family member to describe who I am, they may have an entirely different description. Furthermore, if I were to ask one of my good friends, you might hear yet another story. And for me, that's perfectly fine. The descriptions of my life and me don't define me. As in every living being, I am a flexible and fluid creature. Who I am is changing from moment to moment. Accordingly, the same goes for you.

You might be diabetic today, but that can change tomorrow. What if they find a cure for diabetes? What if you have type 2 diabetes, lose a bunch of weight within a few months, and your pancreas starts working again? Why would you limit yourself to such a description?

When you make the decision to drop your story, your suffering starts to go away. If you're uncertain as to whether or not you do this, watch your words as you talk to others. What are some of the things you say when you meet a person in the first few conversations? You can always tell if someone is living in the past by the first few conversations with them. Once you have clarity on your story and the words you use to describe your life, see how you can rewrite your story if it brings you pain. Finally, know that you *can* rewrite your story.

THE UNDOING OF PARENTAL UPBRINGING

I was 23-years-old when I gave birth to my first child. While I always wanted to be a mom, it was a surprise pregnancy. I was in college and got pregnant while I was breaking up with my boyfriend at the time. As a "good catholic girl" (I write that with a bit of tongue-in-cheek humor), I did the "right thing" and married him. I then had two other wonderful children. Even though you're considered an adult at age twenty-three, I certainly didn't feel like I was done growing. I often say that I grew up while I was raising my daughter. We were learning together. In my growing, I made every mistake in the book when it came to parenting. I often joked that she would need a life-time of therapy to undo all the damage I did. Today I will cut myself a little slack on my parenting skills because I have wonderful kids who magically turned out very well. But I will also report that my eldest child has told me many times all the ways in which I damaged her self-esteem. While I know I made mistakes along the way, I was slightly shocked to hear her interpretation of my parenting. I'll bet your parents feel the same when you criticize what they did or didn't do.

Here's what I would like you to take away from this section. When it comes to healing your past and letting go of pain, you must remember that your parents did the best they could at the time they raised you. If they could have, they would have done better. They did what they could with the resources they had, the emotional intelligence they had, and with the skillset they had at the time. I truly don't believe that any parent goes into parenting and says, "I'm going to find a way to severely emotionally damage my children." Even the most misguided parent who is on drugs and selling their body for sex was doing the best thing they knew to do at the time they were doing it. For one minute, put yourself in the shoes of the parent who was abusive, neglectful, or severe. Even in those extreme cases, (and believe me I am not excusing those types of behavior), can you imagine the pain and suffering they were feeling that caused them to behave in those ways? As a parent, especially a mom, you come hardwired with unconditional love for your child. It's in your DNA. You have to try really hard to overcome those feelings of love or be very mentally ill. So imagine what it takes for a parent to be suffering so much that they take actions to harm their children. It takes an insurmountable amount of pain to supersede the feelings of love you have for your child. Again, please read this emphasis in my message: I am not excusing or advocating bad or abusive behavior at all. I am trying to help you heal your pain without 20 or 30 years of therapy. The parent who mistreated you was severely misguided or abused themselves. The parent who mistreated you may have had an untreated mental illness. Once you're able to truly grasp that, it will help you start moving beyond your pain.

Now let's explore parents who were not abusive in any way, but who may have missed the mark when it came to you and your personality. Many people choose to live in pain from their upbring-ing because they believe their parents should have treated them differently. We all know stories of parents who favor one child over another. Or parents who parented with severe or less severe dis-ciplinary actions based on birth order. The ongoing joke is that by the third child you pretty much give up on rules. (I know that was the case for me.) What happens when you're harboring anger or resentment toward your parents because you wish you would have been treated better?

My advice to you is to first mourn the loss of the childhood you wished you could have had. You can even write a story around it. Yes, you heard me correctly. Give your inner child that fantasy. Rewrite your childhood with a new story. In this story, you get to be the favorite child or the one who got to go to all of the parties, for example. Also, in this story you will have your ideal relationship with both of your parents and even with your siblings. Once you've written your story, reread it, and live it in your mind's eye. Imagine that you actually lived all of the things in your story. Give your inner child that delight. After that, put the new story aside. Then, go to your actual story, the one you lived, and revisit it. Is there anything about that story of your upbringing that you can salvage as being good?

For example, as I have mentioned throughout this book, I lived a very difficult childhood with my mom. She was misguided and angry. However, many times she would try her best. In salvaging parts of my childhood that I can find good here's what I found. My mom made me a bagged lunch every day for school. In this lunch she would often write little notes of encouragement for my day and many times she would include stickers. If I reflect hard, I can find other things that redeem our story so that I can release the pain of a painful childhood. Furthermore, becoming a parent was healing for me. Yet, having a daughter as a first child terrified me. I was terrified that I would turn out like my mother. Through my tragic memories I become cognizant of how not to act. And through the tough times of parenting, I become more compassionate toward my mother and the difficulties she went through. It didn't excuse how she treated me as a child. If I go back to those moments the pain is still there. But instead I choose to focus on the good times and now I look at the person my mother is today. From a mature perspective, I see that my mother is a lost child still stuck in her past. Her own childhood was difficult and I can now have compassion for that inner child. I see that she was confused and hurt and still is today. When I see her from this perspective, it lessens my hurt. And the beauty of forgiveness is that she is a wonderful grandmother. Through the eyes of my children I can see a different side of her that I didn't see when I was a child.

The great part about being an adult is that you get to be your own parent now. You don't have to adhere to the upbringing you were subjected to as a child. And if you're able to look at your upbringing from a more spiritual perspective, your soul chose your parents for a reason. You had lessons you needed to learn. Your character needed to be formed in a specific way for your life path and purpose. If you can't find anything else good about your childhood, cling to your spiritual perspective. *You needed your parents to learn the lessons your soul needed to learn to be the person you are today.* And that is truly all you need to know.

UNPROCESSED FEELINGS ANCHOR YOU TO THE PAST

As we move into letting go of our past and forgiving the people who may have harmed us, we might be haunted by feelings we didn't even know were there. When feelings arise from an event you thought you had long forgotten, that is called unprocessed emotional pain. Unprocessed emotional pain is like a silent killer. It sneaks up on you when you least expect it.

In 2018, I went through a traumatic experience that brought up old wounds from the years 2007-2008. While I can't speak about it in detail here, let's suffice it to say that it involved breaking away from an abusive situation. The experience in 2018, with the same person, brought up emotions and trauma I thought I had resolved. The emotions that burst through during that experience brought me back to the 2007-2008 time-period in my physical body. It wreaked havoc on my emotional state and left me near suicidal. The worst part was that it took me completely by surprise. I'm pretty self-aware and I do a lot of personal healing work. But in retrospect, I believe I dealt with what I could by the end of that time in 2008, and kept the rest bottled up to wrestle with at some other time. Unbeknownst to me, that other time was ten years later. What happened was, the 2018 event brought up enough similarities that triggered the former experience as if I was actually re-living it. Luckily, I had enough of a support network to help me through, but it was not a smooth ride. And if I'm honest, as I'm writing this in 2020, I can tell you that the emotions are not gone at one hundred percent.

Our human brains tend to work that way. When an experience is too traumatic for us to handle, we tend to pack away the unprocessed emotions for a later day. It's a protection mechanism so we don't shut down completely. The other day I was talking with a client who said that she didn't remember most of her childhood. She had an alcoholic father and a completely neglectful mother. As a result, she unconsciously blocked out everything until what she remembers at age sixteen.

The unfortunate part is that those emotions don't just disappear. They come back at some point to be processed. How you process them is the key to moving through them. Sometimes that means you spend some time in psychotherapy. Other times it means you revisit the situation with fresh eyes and process through journaling or another exercise to let go. Whatever the case, as these emotions go unprocessed they can develop into other things such as an autoimmune disease or chronic lifestyle illnesses. You know the expression, upon hearing upsetting news, *I have a pit in my stomach?* Emotions that stay balled up on the inside can and do manifest as physical symptoms.

The great news in dealing with unprocessed emotions is that a meditation practice can kickstart the healing process. As you sit silently to meditate, your subtle body takes the state of silent awareness as the opportunity to have its say. It can be annoying and slightly scary for those who have a lot to process. During this period, which usually includes the first 60 days of silent meditation, I advise my students to write down the emotions that arise. And of course, if the feelings get too intense or unbearable, it's best to seek help from a mental health professional.

The reason why this often happens is because in the hustle and bustle of daily life, we don't frequently take the time to be silent. As a result, even if emotions do come up to be processed, we have a tendency to push them away or worse, don't even notice. Just as you experience a physical detox during the first few weeks of a diet, you go through an emotional detox when you begin your meditation practice. As I mentioned, some people get frightened. They wrongfully believe that the meditation practice is somehow making them crazy. When in reality it's actually making them healthier. It's purging what is no longer needed and working through past issues that have been dormant.

You can store unprocessed emotions in any area of your body. And everyone is different. You can bring awareness to where you store unprocessed emotions by tuning into your body. Where does it hurt when you get stressed? Do you feel it in your neck and shoulders? Do you get digestive disturbances? Or do you get migraines? Some people report that when they get a massage and the therapist hits a certain spot, they start crying. That is an emotional release. The release indicates that they were storing unprocessed emotions in that area of the body.

You might be wondering, "How can I tune into my body to find this information?" You can start by getting quiet and commencing deep belly breathing through the nose. For this I would recommend the 4-4-4 Breath. In this exercise you inhale for the count of four, hold it for four, and exhale for four. Do eight to ten rounds and while your eyes are still closed, begin to observe your body. Where do you feel twinges? Do you feel sharp or dull pain anywhere? In what part or parts of your body do you feel discomfort? Allow your body to speak to you in this way. It will communicate with you. But you need to ask.

As you feel these signals of pain or discomfort, you can mindfully direct the breath to those areas of your body. Then continue to breathe deeply as you feel the release. You can also take it one step further and ask the pain what emotions lie within. If you're reminded of a person, place, or time period, let your mind go to that memory. It's usually an indication that you're moving in the right direction. Always have a journal nearby so you can record your memories and experiences. As you breathe and allow the messages to arise, you'll notice that the pain and discomfort will subside. Depending on the amount of unprocessed emotions that you need to heal, you may have to repeat the exercise several times to feel a sense of resolution.

WHY IT'S SO DIFFICULT TO PROCESS EMOTIONS

In exploring how to take off the masks covering suppressed emotions, let's pinpoint why it's so difficult and often messy to process our emotions.

Human emotions have a depth to them that cannot be confined by set boundaries. Have you ever started to deal with an emotion and in dealing with it, a whole host of other emotions showed up? Then you turn to deal with those and even more surface? In frustration you quit because it seems like a never-ending process. The human mind is messy. And emotions are even messier. Most of us are educated in a system that teaches us well-defined lessons with a set of answers. For example, when you learn algebra, you learn equations and how to solve those equations. Or, when you learn the parts of an earthworm in biology, you learn how to label those parts and they are the same every time with every earthworm. Furthermore, when you learn how to construct a sentence with proper grammar, your teacher will give you a grade based on accuracy according to the rules of grammar. Processing emotions gives you none of that. The complexity of your internal reaction based on something external can change from one situation to the next or from one time period to the next. The unpredictability of emotional processing makes most people run from it.

In the end, this reaction is not surprising. Throughout my life I've read many books on psychology, relationships, and emotional healing. In addressing this issue, two books I've read come to mind, *Emotional Intelligence* by Daniel Goleman and *Non-Violent Communication* by Marshall Rosenberg. Both of these books mention the fact that the constructs of society in the modern world do not teach us from a young age how to deal with emotions. We don't even have an expansive vocabulary for feelings. Even though we have progressed a little in comparison to the 1940s or 1950s, for example, emotional literacy is moving forward at a snail's pace.

You may be wondering how I am judging this progress or how I know. Well, I don't have a degree in rocket science or a PhD in psychology, but it doesn't take a scientist to clearly see that we haven't progressed that far. Let me give you some examples. Addiction to alcohol, drugs, and most importantly to opioids is at an all-time high. In the United States alone, according to the National Institute on Drug Abuse, over 128 people die daily from opioid overdose. Opioid overdose increased over 30% in one year from 2016 to 2017.[7] In addition, according to the National Survey on Drug Use and Health (NSDU) 19.7 million American adults (ages 12 and over) suffered from a substance use disorder in 2017.[8] While alcohol and drug misuse and abuse is a complex topic, I will surmise that those who abuse drugs and alcohol have some emotional issues to sort out. To further this example; written prescriptions related to anxiety and depression are at an all-time high as well. Anxiety disorders affect 40 million American adults each year making it the most common mental illness.[9] Prescriptions for anti-anxiety medications involving benzodiazepines-such as Xanax, Librium, Valium, and Ativan, increased 67% between 1996 and 2013 and have resulted in a four-fold increase in overdoses of these medications since 1999[10].

7   https://www.drugabuse.gov/drugs-abuse/opioids/opioid-overdose-crisis Opioid Overdose Crisis, National Institute on Drug Abuse Feb. 2020

8   "Alcohol and Drug Abuse Statistics," Scot Thomas, MD. American Addiction Centers. Feb. 3, 2020 https://americanaddictioncenters.org/rehab-guide/addiction-statistics

9   "Facts & Statistics," Anxiety and Depression Association of America. https://adaa.org/about-adaa/press-room/facts-statistics

10   "Antianxiety Drugs -- Often More Deadly Than Opioids." Ashleigh Garrison. CNBC. Friday, August 3, 2018.https://www.cnbc.com/2018/08/02/antianxiety-

Heal Yourself: A Return to Wholeness

Even though I believe you might be starting to see the trend of how little we've advanced in our emotional healing, I will give you one more example. According to the World Health Organization, obesity has nearly tripled since 1975. In 2016, more than 1.9 billion adults were overweight and of them over 650 million were obese. In addition, over 40 million children were either overweight or obese in 2018.[11]

All of these statistics show that these behavioral outcomes demonstrate a problem that goes well beyond the occasional drink, pill, or food item to soothe emotional pain. They show a deep unresolved need to understand at a profound level how to manage and process emotions.

But in order to adequately process painful emotions or emotions in general, it's necessary to understand how and why.

REWIRING OUR EMOTIONAL MIND

Have you ever had a thought, let's say about your mother and a certain trait she possesses? In this thought you say to yourself, *I never want to have this trait like my mother. I don't like it. In fact, I hate it and I don't want to have that like her.* In that effort, you keep repeating that thought to yourself for years or decades. What often happens is one day you wake up and notice that you have that exact same trait, the one you were trying to avoid. What in the world happened? Your fluid mind kept entertaining that thought again and again. And over time, it recognized the trait as something familiar. Familiar feels good to the human brain. So you wound up like your mother in some way. Another way you could have trained

drugs-fuel-the-next-deadly-drug-crisis-in-us.html

11   "Obesity and Overweight." World Health Organization. Feb. 16, 2018.
https://www.who.int/health-topics/obesity#tab=tab_1

the mind to have a different outcome would have been to think about an opposite trait. Let's suppose that the trait is, *My mom is always late and I hate that.* (My mother is, in fact, always late.) The fluid mind is better trained with a phrase like, *I'm so grateful that I am always 15 minutes early wherever I go.* Your mind then picks up on *early, early, early* for years. And what do you know? One day you are arriving early to every appointment and meeting.

You are not a byproduct of your genes and upbringing. You are a byproduct of your consistent thoughts, emotions, and behaviors.

Another phrase I consistently heard growing up was, *We are poor.* It didn't matter if it was a time period when we were actually in great need or one during which things got better. That phrase was still omnipresent in the household.

It takes a lot of effort to overcome ingrained phrases from your past. Changing your future counts on a consistent practice of paying attention to your internal dialogue to help overcome phrases that no longer serve who are and who you want to become.

As you retrain your mind to adopt the new evolutionary thoughts, you might be inclined to think that it's just wishful thinking. I've been using the power of positive affirmations for years and I can say with great enthusiasm that it works. In the beginning you will feel like you're lying to yourself. Let's suppose you *are* living in poverty or have a difficult time paying your bills. If you repeat a phrase such as, *Huge amounts of money are flowing into my life every single day*, you might get uneasy. Yet as your brain is rewiring, your central nervous system will be subconsciously searching for a way for new sources of money to come into your life. It's uncanny how that happens.

Repeating positive affirmations also represents something we call faith. Having faith that good things will come to you in turn makes good things come to you. It sounds simplistic but it's true. Have you ever heard of a self-fulfilling prophecy? It happens all the time. People get in a negative mindset and repeat negative phrases endlessly. As a result they see their worst nightmares come true. Well, what if you could have a self-fulfilling prophecy happen, but in the positive? It works the same but the benefit of repeating positive affirmations is that they hold a higher vibration than negative ones. Therefore, you will see your visualizations and affirmations come to fruition sooner rather than later. The reason is that when you repeat positive phrases, you align yourself with the flow of the universe. The universe is creativity and thus in a positive flow. Even in destruction, it still paves the way for rebirth and regrowth.

In conclusion, you're not a prisoner to your past nor are you shackled to your negative thoughts. Both can change with mindfulness in the present and a positive projection toward the future.

YOU GET TO DECIDE WHO YOU ARE NOW

I've coached many people who remain tethered to their past. The stark reality is, you are an adult now and you can exercise your free will. Even though you may not perceive it, you're reinventing yourself constantly. And as a responsible adult, you get to decide who you are each and every day. It's true that you have certain personality traits you must work with and perhaps a small amount of limitations, but all in all you have choices.

I hear many stories of parents who weren't present or who abandoned my clients. I hear stories of divorce, rape, incest, or incarceration. I also hear stories about infidelity, poverty, and drug or alcohol use. In the time I've been doing spiritual counseling, I've heard it all. Those who remain tethered to their past forget one universal truth, *The person you are in the present moment is a choice.* At any given moment you get to choose who you are and how you're going to live your life. Unless you are imprisoned, you have complete power to decide. And even then, I've read stories of prisoners who have transformed their lives from the inside of a prison. Understand that if your life is not going in the direction you want it to go, you are the only one responsible for that. If you're holding onto your past or continuing to blame your parents, grandparents, siblings, or any other loved one for the way you are, you're only leaning on that excuse to not move forward. Moving on is as easy as a decision.

Most successful people I read about came from loads of adversity. My favorite examples are Walt Disney, Oprah Winfrey, Wayne Dyer, Tony Robbins, and Barack Obama. These people didn't have anything extraordinary to start out. They only had willingness, desire, and drive to overcome their past.

CHAPTER FIVE: RECAP OF LESSONS LEARNED

1. Attachment to the past is one of the greatest sources of suffering.

2. Your past and all of the events and people contained within it were designed to teach you something.

3. Remaining in your past causes self-infliction of suffering.

4. Living in the present with a clear view of your future is the best way to minimize suffering and pain. Let the present moment be your anchor.

5. Even if you didn't like your past, you can rewrite your story today.

6. Processing emotions from your past is important for living healthfully today.

7. Positive affirmations can help you rewire your emotional mind.

8. Moving on is as easy as a decision.

SIX

ACCEPT THE NATURE OF DUALITY

Transcendence means going beyond duality. Attachment means remaining in duality. -Rajneesh

Your soul has chosen this lifetime to have an earthly experience. In order to fully embrace this experience with minimal pain, you must accept the parameters of life on Earth. Life for all creatures comes with duality. It's part and parcel of agreeing to be here. The more you accept it, the easier your life will be. The more you resist, the further away you will find yourself from healing and therefore, wholeness.

ACCEPTANCE OF DUALITY

Duality means that everything in life comes with its opposite. You can't have day without night or light without dark. You also can't experience pleasure without first knowing pain. The opposite nature of one allows you to have the experience of the other. How can you know, for example, what it feels like to be energetic unless you've also been tired? You can't.

Oftentimes we squeeze ourselves into a box. In that box we want to only experience good or pleasure, while keeping out the bad or pain. First of all, this is an unrealistic goal. Secondly, as you do that you miss out on a whole portion of life. Here's why; most of our growth comes through suffering or the "bad stuff."

Think back to all of the periods of major growth in your life. Then reflect on the events that happened six to twelve months prior to that growth. Most of the time you'll find that right before your big leap, a huge setback occurred.

When I was a teenager I wanted more than anything to move to California to attend college. I talked about California for years leading up to my senior year in high school. However, my mom did everything in her power to prevent that from happening. As a result I disappointedly started college at The University of Michigan, which was much closer to home. But in my disappointment, I made the decision that I wanted to graduate in three years to get the heck out of Michigan. So after my freshman year, I took the summer term. During that summer, I decided to take a few classes to get rid of my general education requirements. One of the classes I took was French two. My teacher's assistant, who was a master's student, was one of the most motivating teachers I've ever had. During the semester he had a friend visiting from France who came to speak to the class about French culture and the cities of Cannes and Aix-en-Provence, in the South of France. As a result I was motivated to study abroad and found a program starting that fall. I applied, got in, and ended up spending the following four years studying in France, where I had my first child and ended up marrying a French man. While the marriage didn't last, I got my three wonderful children as a result of that marriage. In addition, I had many of the most culturally enhanced and eye-opening experiences of my life traveling through Europe and having the freedom to be in a foreign country on my own. As you can see, my major setback of not being able to follow my initial plan to go to college in California led me to many adventures and the birth of my three children.

Without a doubt, you've intuitively known that life is about balance. As an ancient Vedic saying goes, "Life is a river flowing between the banks of pain and pleasure. You will bump into both sides. But the idea is to not get stuck on one side for too long." Have you ever been moving through life and things were going pretty well? Your life was running smoothly and you seemed to be having great luck. Then suddenly this thought pops into your head and spooks you. *If things are too good, something bad is likely to happen soon.* You might call that superstition or panic. For some people, who live in constant worry, that's sometimes the case. But in reality, based on your life experience you know how things go. Life can only be smooth for a time and then bumps will arrive to create some chaos. These annoyances may be big or small. But your inner knowing says, *Things can't be 100% good all the time.*

And that's the truth of duality. The good news is that you can prepare yourself for obstacles or annoyances. That's why we have things like savings accounts and insurance policies. However, some things in life come to us rather unexpected. At that point you have a choice as to how you're going to react. Some people simply don't want to accept duality as reality.

Those who can't accept the nature of duality have a tendency to feel great when life is going well and shocked when it isn't. The more you can learn to accept life's challenges, the less pain you'll experience. Life is about fun, joy, and laughter, but it's also about flat tires, economic downturns, and relationships that go sour. Since everything is constantly changing, nothing lasts forever. The person who is best able to stay even-keeled when the storms arise is usually the happiest and healthiest.

I know people who believe their lives are completely over when they lose a job or a spouse leaves them. While it's important to process pain and loss, you must not remain in that space. You must be able to find joy within the pain in order to temper your reaction to life's events.

As one of my favorite YouTuber's, Justin Scarred, says, "You can't control your circumstances but you *can* control your reaction to them." Similarly I'm reminded of the *Serenity Prayer* used in 12-Step groups worldwide that reads:

> *God, grant me the serenity to accept the things I cannot change.*
> *The courage to change the things I can,*
> *And the wisdom to know the difference.*

The main reason you're likely to feel upset when obstacles arrive is because you feel out of control. Obstacles bring about the unknown and you can't always see the outcome. It's at those moments that it's best to keep your eye on the bigger picture, stay grounded in your higher spiritual self, and surrender to your higher power.

REMAINING IN NON-JUDGMENT

As we unpack this topic, I'd like to first define the word *judgment*. According to Dictionary.com, *judgment* means, "the ability to judge, make a decision, or form an opinion objectively, authoritatively, and wisely, especially in matters affecting action; good sense; discretion." It further notes, "the forming of an opinion, estimate, notion, or conclusion, as from circumstances presented to the mind."

If a judge in the court of law is fair, they weigh out all of the facts presented and make an assessment based on an objective truth. However, you know as well as I do that a judgment doesn't always represent the truth in a court case. But legal systems in democracies around the world have strived, nonetheless, to make judgments as close to the truth as they can.

In the late 20th and early 21st century I'm sure you've noticed that one big phrase of political correctness is, "Don't judge!" Or, "Don't judge me!" The truth is everyone judges to some extent. It's in our nature. If you never judge, that is, if you never form an opinion based on circumstances presented to your mind, you will never, ever make any decision. And that can be dangerous.

Let's suppose you're in a new city trying to find the closest coffee shop. As your phone's GPS takes you to a street corner, you notice a group of young men with chains on their pants, smoking, and talking loudly. You observe that they kick trashcans as they walk by and push each other into the street jokingly. In your observation you may, on one hand think, *They're just kids and probably harmless.* On the other hand your intuition tells you, *Maybe you should avoid them and walk down another street.* Based on this judgment call, you turn and walk the other way. Now what if I told you that those kids also happened to be African-American? Would that make you racist or judgmental based on their skin color? Maybe and maybe not. Now suppose these kids are Caucasian. Does that make you less judgmental? All you were doing was making a judgment call for your own safety based on a set of circumstances before you. No matter what the color, race, or ethnicity of the kids in this example, imagine you hadn't listened to your intuition and had walked through the group of kids. Perhaps nothing would have happened. But what if you were mugged or roughed up instead? The truth is, in avoiding the scene you never found out. However, your judgment call was in place designed to keep you safe.

If anyone ever tells you, "I don't judge." Rest assured they are lying. Every time you shun a pizza restaurant over another, you're making a judgment. If you deem wearing jeans to work on casual Fridays is dressing down too much, you're making a judgment. Do you see? It's not bad. It's just a normal part of life.

The problem with judgment comes when we make an assessment based on something superficial or by not having all the facts. Judgment also creates problems when we create over-generalizations based on gross exaggerations. Some examples include:

All men are pigs.

Women are fickle.

Politicians are liars.

The world is a bad place.

All the good men are taken.

By these examples you can hopefully see that the problem here doesn't lie in judgment. The problem lies in over-generalizing an entire group of people based on a concept that may or may not be true for some. Sometimes these are referred to as stereotypes.

If you can wholly embrace the concept of duality, you come the conclusion that the potential for good and bad exist in everyone. Take for example the actor and comedian, Bill Cosby. I grew up watching the Cosby show, hearing the voice of Bill Cosby on the animated television series *Fat Albert,* and later introduced Cosby to my kids and even saw his stand up show one year in the early 2000s. A few years back, the news featured story after story of how Cosby continually drugged and sexually abused women throughout his career and in 2018 was found guilty of three accounts of sexual assault.[12] On one hand, we can see a man who brought joy to millions for decades and on the other hand, we see a sinister and disturbed man with psychotic behavior that showed up behind the scenes. If you grew up a fan of Cosby like me, hearing news like that was shocking and horrifying. But it does demonstrate duality at its finest. Each person has the potential for great good and extreme evil.

Remaining in a state of non-judgment simply means taking the stance, *Maybe I don't know enough to see the bigger picture.* Sometimes you do know enough and can make a sound judgment. But sometimes you don't and remaining in non-judgment is the best way to broaden your field of vision.

ACCEPT YOUR LIGHT & DARK SIDE

Having been raised Roman Catholic; I had a lot of guilt surrounding many aspects of my life. Remaining in non-judgment of yourself is difficult when you are constantly being told, "God will punish you if..." The parameters in strict religious practices whether you're catholic, protestant Christian, Muslim, Jewish, Hindu, or any other religion can cause your darker side to sink deep into the shadows. When I was a teenager, I was very rebellious. In fact, I found that my catholic school classmates possessed behavior that was well over the top when it came to *sex, drugs,* and *rock and roll.* My friends who attended public school, in many ways, behaved much

12   "Bill Cosby Convicted on Three Counts of Sexual Assault." Manuel Rolg-Franzia. Washington Post. April 26, 2018. https://www.washingtonpost.com/lifestyle/style/bill-cosby-convicted-on-three-counts-of-sexual-assault/2018/04/26/d740ef22-4885-11e8-827e-190efaf1f1ee_story.html

better. The restrictions placed on teenagers, or anyone for that matter, to artificially suppress potentially "bad behavior" actually causes those bad behaviors to surface more. I've often heard the expression, *What you resist, persists.* For example, if you keep telling your teenager, with a budding curiosity about sexuality, "You can't have sex until you're married. It's forbidden," what is the first thing they're going to want to do? While sex doesn't have to be shadow energy, by making it bad or forbidden, you can easily propel it into that darker form.

The same goes for any behavior that you push into the dark. For example, you might say to yourself after gaining several pounds, *I'm never eating chocolate again!* Yet after a few days, you may find yourself searching the house obsessively to find a small piece of chocolate.

You don't necessarily have to be restricted or suppressed to have shadow traits. Everyone has something that makes them feel shameful or embarrassed at times. It could be that you're impatient or get angry quickly. Or perhaps you are deeply insecure or have a difficult time in social situations. These traits are often accompanied by the internal dialogue, *I wish I was more like...Or, I wish I could change this about me.*

What I've found is that by embracing your shadow or darker energy, it naturally dissipates. When you brush it under the rug, it tends to get stronger because pushing it away gives it more energy. Invite your shadow energy in. Observe it without judgment.

Most people have a difficult time admitting they have a shadow side. They claim, "I'm a good person and I do good things." While that may be true, everyone has a counterbalance to their good or favorable traits. Those who are the healthiest mentally are able to see that balance. They're able to recognize where they fall short or in what areas of their lives they'd like to improve.

When it comes to your emotional life, many would rather not have the experience of negative emotions. In fact, most people fight against them. And it's in fighting against negative emotions that shadows tend to develop. These shadows become behavioral patterns such as: people pleasing, addictive behaviors, unhealthy coping mechanisms, enabling, or denying one's own needs. When we refuse to experience emotional pain and admit our weaknesses, we block ourselves off from ourselves.

I believe the best modern explanation of the balance between light and dark comes from the notion of the *Jedi* in Lucas Film's *Star Wars*. In the first six *Star Wars* movies you get a lighter description of Jedi knights, but in the more recent trilogy starting with *The Force Awakens* the writers emphasize the delicate balance of force energy. Being a yogi, I was amused at the rather yogic explanation that the retired Jedi, Luke Skywalker, gives to budding Jedi, Rey. Skywalker points out that a thin line exists between light and dark and that everyone has the potential to choose or cross the line too far into the other side. Rey expands this notion as she continually tries to save Kylo Ren stating throughout the films, *I still see good in him.*

While we tend to categorize people as either good or bad, the truth is a thin line does exist. And those who are on either side of the spectrum can easily fall to either extreme. Health and healing are about walking the thin line of balance.

PAIN AS YOUR GURU

Let's get specific as we talk about pain. I don't adhere to the common catch phrase in sports, "No pain, no gain!" In order to disperse our shadow energy, we need to learn to move toward pain and address it.

In this book our main focus is on emotional pain. Even if pain is physical, however, it's a great messenger that something is off. It's a signal to tune within. When I teach yoga, I always invite my students to differentiate between pain and discomfort. The moment you ease your body into a posture or hold a yoga pose, for example, it's normal to experience discomfort. In a yoga asana, you're stretching muscles, ligaments, and fascia that may need to be stretched, so you will feel something. What's not normal, however, is to experience sharp pain. Pain in yoga indicates that you're doing something wrong or pushing yourself too hard. Discomfort should be invited in during a physical practice, whereas pain is a warning.

The same parameters can be applied to your emotions. Stretching yourself to feel a feeling may cause discomfort, but when we ignore our feelings we usually start to experience pain. As a result of ignoring our feelings over days, weeks, months, and years, we have an accumulation of pain that must be addressed if we are to heal. And that's what I mean when I refer to pain as your guru.

The word *guru* is a Sanskrit word that translates to "dispeller of darkness." Most people know of the darkness that comes when we are in an emotional funk. Steeped in deep negative emotions, you often cannot eat, sleep, or even function properly. Let's learn how to use your pain as a guru.

YOUR SHADOW: A MASK FOR PAIN

Healing yourself comes first by unmasking your pain. "What?" You may protest, "I don't mask my pain!" In response I will give you one example only because I believe we've all done this at least once. Have you ever eaten something to forget about an emotion? It could have been heartbreak, a bad grade on a test, getting into a fight with a friend, finding out your work colleague got the promotion instead of you, or anything else. My guess is that you've done this at least once in your life. You've eaten away your pain in some shape or form. Now let's extend that example to drinking alcohol, taking a pill, or using a drug. If the previous examples are not your escape methods of choice, how about emotional shopping or excessive game playing? Have you ever used any type of distraction to try and push away emotional pain? We've all done it. The problem is not, *have you done it once?* The question that remains is *how often have you done it?*

Where do you think those emotions have gone? They haven't just disappeared on their own. Suppressed emotions and unprocessed pain sink deep into your cells and subconscious mind to be dealt with at a later time. In healing yourself, the time is now. It's time to take off the masks that have kept your emotions hidden if you are to heal.

WHEN A GOOD THING BECOMES A SHADOW

In addition, some people even perceive positive emotions as pain. For example, having a person fall in love with you can represent pain or a negative feeling even though the feeling of love is inherently positive. The example of falling in love may hit close to home, so let's dig deeper into this good thing that can become a shadow.

Love is a natural trait for all of us. Our true nature is love. As beings of love, it's what we all crave. However, many of us have had less than optimal experiences when it comes to love. Caregivers, other family members, and friends may have shown us varying degrees of love. Or perhaps we didn't receive love in the way that speaks to our love language.

When it comes to romantic love, negative experiences can lead to pushing this basic human need into the shadows. Most people crave romantic love. This craving, which comes from a need, causes people to go out and search for a romantic partner. Yet in the confusion of where love sits on their personal spectrum, many can then send confusing messages to those they seek out for love. Let me illustrate.

Perhaps you've been hurt many times in love. As a result, the realm of romantic relationships has been pushed into the shadows. But because you have a driving desire to love and be loved, you get on a few dating sites and start dating. In the first few dates you find that the early stages of relationship are easy, but as time goes on and the words "love" or "relationship" enter the picture, you find yourself running away. If you have not done this, do you know anyone who has?

I already mentioned that love is who we are as humans. Love is inherent in our nature. We are created to connect and create loving relationships. How does something so good and needed get pushed so deeply into the shadows?

It all comes down to unprocessed pain. In reality, anything good can be pushed into shadow energy. One of the most unfortunate things that gets pushed into the shadows is love.

By keeping love in the shadows, not only do you deprive yourself from love, but you also create rifts in current relationships by ping-ponging back and forth. You need love and therefore move toward other humans, then you are pulled back by your shadow that says, *Love is bad. Love hurts you. Love makes you too vulnerable and open to wounds.* To that end you remain in pain.

MOVE TOWARD PAIN, SUFFERING, & YOUR SHADOW

Heal Yourself: A Return to Wholeness

The wound is the place where Light enters you. -
Rumi

In reality, we cannot truly mask pain, nor can we ignore it. The only way to properly process emotional pain is to move through it. The last thing you probably want to do is move toward your pain. Yet as the Rumi quote suggests, it's in moving toward that pain that you will find the light within you.

Throughout my life, I've had many occasions to address my wounds and insecurities. However, I believe the greatest and most healing experience came once I met my twin flame. In my book *Twin Flame Romance: The Journey to Unconditional Love*, I explain further how the awakening through meeting your twin flame causes you to uncover your hidden wounds. Like any soulmate relationship, a twin flame is put on Earth to teach you many lessons. Because you are twin souls (in other words, you share a soul split in two), meeting your twin flame ignites mirroring of pain and wounds. As a result you have no other choice than to face your deepest shadows.

You may not be a twin flame or have a soulmate in your life currently, but that doesn't mean you can't face your shadow energy head on. It's true that we learn more about ourselves in relationships than we do alone. Be that as it may, you know to some extent, what wounds and insecurities lie deep within. And if you have a deep, driving desire to heal, you can begin the process of addressing your shadows and greet them like an old friend.

Here are a few examples of ways to start meeting your shadow energy head on.

1. Physical activity

You can start by doing this in the most literal sense. And that is why many people find it useful to move through pain by doing a physical activity such as running.

When I was at the height of puberty as a freshman in high school, my mom forced me to join a sport. The only thing I could do other than dance was swim. So I joined the swim team. Even though I was horrible at it, I was thankful for the hour-long practices every day after school. As you probably remember, being a teenager comes with loads of hormones and a sea of emotions. I distinctly remember that the twenty-lap warm-up in the Olympic-sized pool was my therapy in high school. With the ups and downs of teenage romance, I was a hot mess most of the time. But physical activity kept me sane, as I was able to sort out my feelings through laps in a pool.

2. *Therapy*

I wholeheartedly believe that therapy has its place. It certainly helped me in my early years of adulthood and on several occasions in romantic relationships. If you find it difficult to process painful emotions on your own because you are overwhelmed, I would highly recommend that you start with therapy.

3. *Journaling*

Even if you don't have a habit of writing anything down, keeping a daily journal is extremely helpful. When thoughts are stuck in your head, it can be difficult to process them. You might notice that when you're caught up in stressful thoughts, it seems like a never-ending cycle. Getting thoughts out on paper or on your electronic device helps stop the repetitive cycle even if you aren't able to resolve anything. The other great thing about journaling is that you can look back at your progress and thought patterns throughout time. I don't often reread my journals, but when I do I'm always surprised to see my progress and maturity as time goes on.

4. *Meditation and free-flowing contemplation*

The best resolutions come to us when we're not doing anything in particular. I've addressed the topic of meditation several times throughout this book. And hopefully I've convinced you of its value. Free-flowing contemplation is like daydreaming. In today's busy world we don't often take the time to allow our thoughts to flow. In the days before hand-held electronic devices, we would spend lapses of time during which we'd have periods of silence. For example, if you were driving alone to another state or region and only had a radio to keep you entertained, when the reception got bad you had no other choice than to drive in silence. Letting your mind wander without a particular agenda can actually help you solve problems. Have you ever noticed that your best thoughts come to you in the shower or while doing the dishes? In the beginning of this book I introduced the concept of ego consciousness. As you drift into free-flowing contemplation the ego lets go and allows your spiritual self to emerge. When this happens you open yourself up to infinite possibilities including creative solutions to your problems.

5. *Give your shadow an avatar*

In 2017, I attended Tony Robbin's live event called *Unleash the Power Within*. Even though I had been through many self-help and self-actualization events in the past, this event awoke a new power within me. One of the exercises during the event was a creative technique to address your deepest fears. I believe it's a technique in neurolinguistic programming, but in any case it was genius. Basically, the reason why we have fears of people or events is because we attach a particular emotion to them. But if we change the sensory perception and the emotion surrounding the person or event, we can change the memory attached to it. During the exercise, Tony had us change the visuals or sounds surrounding the trigger event. As we did this, the intensity surrounding the emotional event diminished the more we recalled it. While the exercise was helpful, I had forgotten all about it for a while.

Recently my sister helped me with a problem I had that was triggering me. I had been dealing with a certain person who wanted to push my buttons. Every time I spoke to this person, they threatened to call a lawyer. For me, it created a lot of pain because in my mind, getting a lawyer meant lack of communication and diplomacy and loss of a lot of money. The reason it worked to trigger me every time was because I had all negative associations surrounding lawyers. When I recounted my pain to my sister, she suggested I change the meaning surrounding the word "lawyer." She offered, "What if you imagine Conrad the Unicorn each time this person says 'lawyer' to you? Puzzled, I told her I had no idea who Conrad the Unicorn was. To that end she sent me a picture and I actually laughed out loud. From that point forward it changed my neuro-association to the word "lawyer" and helped release my fear. She had actually used Tony's technique on me without knowing it.

In the same way, you can also assign an avatar to your deepest fears. Change the size, color, smell, or persona of your fear. You will see how much it helps in diffusing its impact on you and your life.

Heal Yourself: A Return to Wholeness

As you might have guessed, healing your shadow energy doesn't take place overnight. Oftentimes the wounds that cause the shadows to lurk in the darkness of our lives are too great to be dealt with at once. But the more you familiarize yourself with your shadows, the easier it will be to obtain the balance you seek. With each visit, those shadows will shrink down to a tolerable size and you can then look at them face to face.

CHAPTER SIX: RECAP OF LESSONS LEARNED

1. Acceptance of the nature of duality gives you a smoother experience of life.

2. If you look back throughout your life, you will find that the most growth happened in periods of adversity.

3. Looking at your shadows is as important as looking at your light.

4. Judgment becomes dangerous only when we overgeneralize or make an assessment based on a lack of facts.

5. Living a balanced life is being able to walk the fine line between light and dark.

6. Healing yourself comes first by unmasking your pain.

7. The only way to properly process emotional pain is to move through it.

SEVEN

SEPARATENESS TO EXPERIENCE ONENESS

Mastering others is strength. Mastering yourself is true power. —Lao Tzu

A s I mentioned in previous chapters, for some of us who are born awakened, the greater problem is not the constricted confines of the ego, but the lack of well-defined boundaries between others and the self. In saying the word *awakened*, I'm not indicating a sense of superiority to any other person. For this discussion, let's equate the word *awakened* to *aware*. Some people are born with an intense awareness that they are spiritual beings. They *know* somehow that we are all connected to infinite Source. These beings can be referred to as highly sensitive individuals, empaths, or in new age circles, lightworkers or Earth angels. These highly spiritually attuned people embark on this life's journey innocent and unaware of the harsh realities of the ego. They are eager to trust and are inherently open and kind.

The reality, that they tend to learn quickly, is that not everyone is operating from spirit. In fact, ego-consciousness is more the norm in this current lifetime. Therefore, these sensitive beings find themselves easily hurt, misunderstood, and labeled as weird or eccentric. Those with strong ego agendas seek out these beings to take advantage of them. Oftentimes, the spiritually aware become doormats as their vulnerability and openness turn into servitude.

As one who is spiritually aware, I don't like to use the term *victim*. While certain situations call for this term, most don't. When you're a child and don't know any better or don't have adequate parental protection, victim can be a good description of a situation in which another person or group of people take advantage of you. But once you become an adult, along with the world of information that we have at our fingertips in the 21st Century, using the word "victim" can be a copout for taking responsibility for yourself and your situation. In addition to being fully spiritually aware, I am also a realist. To that end, I understand that in certain parts of the world, people are indeed victimized based on their gender, religion, social rank or status, and socioeconomic level. Tragedy based on the ego agenda of others is real. We must not turn a blind eye to those realities. However, if you are living in a free world with freedom of speech, movement, and expression, you have a choice toward empowerment.

For those who come hardwired into the world with an attitude of "everything is one" and "there are no boundaries between us," in order for you to heal, you must let go of this concept for now. We must apply the saying attributed to Hippocrates, *Physician heal thyself,* first. You are of no use to anyone, including your friends, family, community, and the planet if you are suffering or living in pain.

HOW THE AWAKENED CAN TAKE ON MORE EGO

Everything in life is about balance. Coming into the world as a highly intuitive and spiritually sensitive human can be jarring when reality hits. As one who is spiritually aware, you are open, trusting, caring, and at times selfless. You would give the shirt off your back to someone in need. In your worldview as, *We are one*, your perception is that everyone understands the laws of spirit. To that end, you expect others to respond in like kind. When they don't you are shocked. Because most spiritually aware people are also empaths, they pick up on others' emotions. Those with a normal or inflated sense of ego might be carrying around low self-esteem, shame, sadness, and anger as a result of being confined by the ego. As a spiritually sensitive person, when others don't respond to you in a way you know is right according to spiritual laws, you turn their actions and reactions back on yourself. Consequently, you ponder things like:

What did I do wrong?
Did I say something that hurt them?
What could I have done differently?
Maybe I should have given more.
Perhaps I need to go and apologize.

The reality is you were acting in spirit, the other person's response was in ego, and yet you expected them to respond in spirit. There is nothing more to that story.

As a result, throughout time you continue to blame yourself because you don't understand how people can act through the lens of the ego. The reason is because you have an *underdeveloped ego*. Let's suppose that throughout your lifetime you encounter all sorts of people who respond to you in this way. Accordingly, you begin to doubt your approach to others. You question yourself more. Then, at a certain point, something happens. You snap. You become passive aggressive, sulky, and start to get manipulative. You start to lie or conceal your true self.

In chapter two, I spoke about stacking pain. When you stack pain, it can translate into cruel behavior. For the spiritually aware, stacked pain doesn't frequently come out as outright cruelty. But it does come out as manipulation. Since you haven't learned to use the ego to serve you in a proper way, you have a difficult time asserting your will or telling others your needs. Let me illustrate by example.

You have a girlfriend who has a fairly "healthy" ego. Every Sunday you meet with her for brunch. You, being the accommodating sensitive soul, let her choose the place. Even though she has politely offered you the choice, which you have declined regularly, she's more than happy to choose. Being that she is a woman with fancy tastes, she's constantly choosing restaurants that are way outside of your budget. In an effort to be a good boyfriend, you offer to pay for her meal every time. Instead of telling her that you really can't afford it or that it stresses you out to see your savings go down, you suck it up and don't tell her anything. Then one day you get fed up. As it gets closer to the weekend, you tell her that you're busy on Sunday morning but that you'll see her later. Then the next week, you offer to make her Sunday brunch at your apartment. When she declines, confused that you don't want to meet with her at her favorite place, you tell her the food made you sick last time.

Do you see that instead of being truthful and seeing to it that your needs are met, you are circumventing the problem to try and accommodate? But in the end it's just manipulation. You are manipulating your girlfriend by making her believe that you can afford these fancy brunches every week, but that you just don't want to go. Because highly sensitive people tend to lack this balance, they often come off as having an even greater ego issue than those who have normally sized egos.

THE GIVE, GIVE, GIVE, TO DEPLETION PROBLEM

One other common trait of the underdeveloped ego as a result of growing up spiritually awakened, is the giver syndrome. If you're this person you know what it's like. You give to everyone you know, even to your detriment. Your personal relationships are often uneven and imbalanced. In these relationships you find that you're constantly the one who is giving money, time, effort, and emotional support and the other person is all about taking it freely. It seems that the more you give, the more they take. Your internal spiritual self knows that the laws of the universe say that life is about give *and* take. While you love to give and as a spiritually awakened person it's in your nature to give, you also have human needs. In the course of these relationships, after some time, you find yourself frustrated and even angry. When you reach your wits end, you find yourself blowing up at the other person or withdrawing completely.

Let's analyze what has happened here and what will continue to happen if you don't change.

1. You have failed to follow the laws of nature.

The laws of nature include balance, the nature of duality, and therefore, the balance of giving and receiving. This balance doesn't mean that giving and receiving will always be 50/50 in equal measure. However, it does mean that when you average out giving and receiving it is more or less even. Everything in the universe takes a big inhalation and exhalation as it flows. For example, deciduous trees will grow and blossom in the spring and their leaves will fall in the autumn. Then the same tress will remain dormant for 4 to 5 months before active regrowth. Here's another example, nocturnal animals will only come out to hunt at night while diurnal animals will hunt by day. Thus, remains the balance of giving and receiving. When you are giving, giving, and giving to depletion, you are disobeying the natural laws of nature. The snapback you feel will come in the way of failed relationships, anger, frustration, depression, or even financial downfall.

2. *You have failed to set healthy boundaries.*

Earth's laws call for boundaries. To a spiritually enlightened person, boundaries don't make sense. Since spirit is spaceless, timeless, and boundless, it goes against everything you intuitively feel. Your internal voice says, "We are all one." Yet in your agreement to live on Earth, you've also agreed to live with boundaries. The human body is a boundary. Your home is a boundary and your workspace is also a boundary. When you conduct your personal relationships according to spiritual laws only, you are disobeying Earthly laws. To live a healthful life, you must set healthy boundaries with others. For example, lending money to a friend, colleague, or family member who has proven untrustworthy to repay you is showing your lack of boundaries to keep you and your finances safe. Let me give you another example. Have you ever had a friend who is consistently calling you complaining about their life? And when you try to reciprocate by sharing, they turn it back to their problems as if they are more important than yours? The unevenness of that relationship is a good reason to either end it or modify it so that you are no longer harming your mental health.

Many empaths or spiritually awakened people have a difficult time telling others that they need to let them go. A great way to do this without being hurtful is to allow God to do the work for you. One day I was watching a show on how great leaders make decisions. Successful leaders seem to consistently make better decisions than those of us who aren't as successful. In this documentary I heard Oprah Winfrey say something like (and I am paraphrasing), "When someone asks me something and I'm not sure what my answer will be, I tell them I'm going to pray about it and get back to them."

Setting boundaries with others doesn't have to be a big affair all the time. And you don't need to make a great announcement, "I'm setting a boundary here people!" You can simply back away from those who aren't serving your highest good. In addition, you can tell the other person, "Hey, I'm making some changes in my life and I'm praying about it. I need to take a time-out from our relationship now so I can get clarity on what I want." Then, and here's the most important piece, *follow through*. Most people, who have a healthy sense of human interaction, will respect you for taking time for yourself. Furthermore, it will also flesh out the people in your life who are really unhealthy. Those people will put up great resistance to your boundaries. They will fight and pursue you. They may even sweet-talk you until you become their friend or lover again. Don't fall for it. If your inner gut feeling has told you that you needed to set that healthy boundary, stick with it. Healthy people will respect healthy boundaries. And highly sensitive and awakened individuals need more, not less, healthy people in their lives.

3. You have failed to love and respect yourself first.

From 2013 to 2018, I was in a romantic relationship with a man who suffered from a severe case of alcoholism and drug addiction. While he concealed his drug addiction from me for over a year, the alcoholism was pretty apparent after the first month. I fell head over heels for him and I know he genuinely loved me too. He was just sick. Knowing absolutely nothing about the disease of alcoholism, I made every single mistake in the book. Even after learning about it and writing a book about it, *Help! I Think My Loved One Is an Alcoholic: A Survival Guide for Lovers, Family, & Friends*, I'm embarrassed to say that I was still caught in the web of the unhealthy relationship. Throughout the years I did learn to set boundaries. And I also learned to surrender to God and not get so crippled by his disease. But I couldn't get away. He and I share a special soulmate connection, so I'm sure you can imagine how hard it was to try and end it. In my delusion over the power of the disease of alcoholism, I truly thought I could *love him* into sobriety. Once I moved to California in 2018 and created some physical distance from him, I slowly learned that the reason I let the relationship run me was that I wasn't loving myself enough. Even though I knew intellectually that I deserved to have a healthy relationship with a man who was healthy, I didn't truly believe it. Now I do. But I had to find the place within me, where I was absolutely fine being by myself. Most importantly, I had to create a loving space for myself to only let in a man who is healthy.

Coming into the Earth awakened, you are used to being loved by your Creator. You know what heavenly love feels like. You are constantly reminded of the omnipresence of love. Having to learn to love yourself is a foreign concept because in the heavenly realms you never felt unloved. To the spiritually aware, self-love can almost feel, well, selfish. So many shy away from the concept of self-love because it seems icky. Your lesson, my dear awakened one, just like my lesson, is to learn with every fiber of your being, how to love yourself completely and this includes accepting yourself. Your body and your physical world need balance. Embracing your dualistic nature is not selfish; it's necessary.

What sometimes happens with enlightened people learning to love themselves and set boundaries is that they become like an emotional kindergartner. The awkwardness that comes with this newfound realization can feel like you're in the playground dividing up toys or M & M candies to make sure they're even. Cut yourself some slack and know that it takes time to get it right. Balance will come more naturally with practice.

Loving yourself completely and with full awareness will also help you when it comes to letting go of the need for approval from others. Let's explore why spiritually awakened people struggle a lot with needing approval and what they can do to recognize and overcome it.

LETTING GO OF THE NEED FOR APPROVAL

An important emotional human need is the need for acceptance. We all need to feel accepted into our family, friends, tribe, and community. Part of that need to be included and accepted is to have the approval of others. In essence, what approval is supposed to mean is that you accept me for who I am, flaws and all. That is what we all crave.

Yet many give up the freedom of who they are for fear that they won't be accepted. Therefore, they change their behavior to seek approval from others. At times we all do this. For example, when you start a new job, you may want to impress your boss and co-workers. So you work hard to prove that they made the right choice. In a sense, that's a healthy way (with a healthy dose of ego) to show you're a team player and that you're serious about your new job. However, when it becomes a constant goal to seek approval in your job, for example, it shows you can't stand on your own two feet. If you need a daily pat on the back, it displays a lack of intrinsic motivation. Because what happens when a day goes by and no one acknowledges you? And what happens when you don't receive recognition for a whole week? Here's what will happen, you'll lack the self-confidence necessary to keep moving forward.

People who come hardwired into this world with a nice big ego and those of us with an underdeveloped ego can experience the same need for approval. However, spiritually awakened people tend to have a harder time and try even more to be accepted. A perfectly logical reason for this exists.

When you come into the world spiritually awake, you also get the gift of being extra empathic. That means you walk into a room and soak up everyone's feelings, emotions, and vibes. Already, you're a highly sensitive individual and by nature, you're also soaking up everyone else's energy. It can become overwhelming. But instead of understanding that you're absorbing someone else's negative "stuff", you have a tendency to mix up their emotions with your own or feel a sense of negativity relating to you. Then you become insecure. The mantra of the spiritually awakened person then tends to be, "Why do they hate me?" Suddenly, every look or hushed word becomes confirmation that you must try harder or be nicer to turn around their opinion of you.

Now let me help you decipher between those with large egos who do this and those with diminished egos who do this. Those with large egos think, "Oh my God, they're talking about me. Those horrible sons of bitches. I'll show them that I'm better." And those with diminished egos (a.k.a. spiritually sensitive) say, "Oh my God, what did I do wrong? Why do they hate me? What can I say to make them like me again? What can I do to set things right? Maybe I'll bake everyone cookies and invite them to a BBQ this weekend." Both are rather ego-based, but the source or the root comes from two different places. In this example, both sets of people are thinking with error that they are the center of the universe. That's ego behavior. But the spiritually sensitive *wants* unity, craves unity, and will do everything in their power to bring about harmony. However, what the spiritually awakened person fails to realize is the difference between a person who is forming an opinion of them and a person who is suffering and wrapped up in themselves.

The empathic person must then decide, *What is yours and what is mine?* Otherwise they become a mess of emotions. If they fail to decipher between their own and others' emotions, they will continue to believe that everyone hates them.

If I were to look back at my childhood, I was pretty well liked as a child. I had good friends who genuinely liked me. But for most of my childhood, up until age 15 or 16, I was convinced that pretty much everyone hated me or didn't like me. I am highly empathic but as a child or even young adult, I had no idea I was constantly absorbing everyone else's negative energy. So I carried around this ball of negative energy and was convinced that it was all pointed toward me. It wasn't until I become an adult and began the pursuit of spiritual teachings that I heard a phrase, "No one is actually thinking about you. They're too tied up in thinking about themselves." In other words, every time you think someone is thinking or talking about you, you're probably wrong. Because they too are thinking, *Oh my God, is that person talking about me or saying something bad about me?* Usually it's not true. Most people are just tied up in their own stuff.

What it comes down to is, you have to like you for who you are. You have to find enough love for your individual self and strengthen your self-confidence so you don't need the approval of others. One hundred people could be sitting in a room with you and have a hundred different opinions about you. In truth, none of that matters. Your opinion of yourself is the only one that truly matters. Remember the lesson from the previous chapter? *Who is the only person you must wake up to every morning of your life?* The answer is you. *And who is the only person you must go to sleep with every night?* The answer is the same, you. People will come and go in your life. But if you can't love yourself unconditionally, you're going to have a difficult time integrating into the collective seamlessly.

CHAPTER SEVEN: RECAP OF LESSONS LEARNED

1. Those who are born spiritually awakened might have an underdeveloped ego.

2. Unbeknownst to them, the spiritually aware can easily become doormats for those who have a healthy or inflated ego.

3. These spiritually aware individuals are also referred to as awakened, empaths, lightworkers, sensitive souls, or Earth Angels.

4. Because spiritually sensitive individuals come from a place of unity, they have a difficult time understanding how to live with separateness.

5. Learning to take on some ego voluntarily is a healthy way to create boundaries and assert will and desire.

6. The laws of nature create a need for a balance between ego and spirit when it comes to expressing yourself in the outer world.

7. Learning how to love yourself unconditionally, including every aspect of yourself, is the ongoing work of the spiritually awakened person.

EIGHT

THE RESURGENCE OF THE SELF

Health is the greatest possession. Contentment is the greatest treasure. Confidence is the greatest friend. Non-being is the greatest joy. —Lao Tzu

Returning to wholeness is an amazing awakening to the truth. You're finally remembering your true nature. With this knowledge you feel liberated and more aligned. Even though this new awareness feels familiar, it also feels uncertain because the territory seems unknown. Depending on how many years you've lived before this discovery, you've spent a fair amount of time in ego-based consciousness or in emotional turmoil based on fear. The law of familiarity says repeated behaviors become ingrained over time. As such, those behaviors become the most familiar. And your mind tends to like familiar. It feels comforting and real. Yet, your newfound shift into operating from your higher spiritual self, while it's liberating, can also feel awkward. Those who are newly awakened to the enlightened path revert easily and often back to old behaviors. Operating from a sense of wholeness, with full awareness, takes time and patience.

Imagine the groves on a vinyl record. They are ingrained in a certain pattern where a song is recorded. Your brain has similar groves where your memories are recorded. The more you've repeated a behavioral pattern, the deeper the groves are imbedded in your memory. Therefore, in the same way, it takes time to create new patterns so that new neurological connections are recorded. But rest assured, with practice they will be.

The more you practice silence, meditation, witnessing awareness, and observation, the more the neuro-pathways will strengthen in the areas of the prefrontal cortex and other areas in the brain that take you away from the ancient limbic system responses. The more you practice love instead of fear, the more you will connect to your higher spiritual self and feel more empathy, compassion, and love for others. And the more you take a step back and not respond with the ego, the more you will reach creative solutions that will bring about unity rather than separation and dissonance.

The resurgence of your newfound self, the integrated one in harmony with your body, mind, emotions, soul, and spirit, can call for tools to remain in wholeness. In the following sections, we will explore these tools. Healing is an ongoing process. We are never a finished product. With each layer of growth comes new growth and healing. However, if you remain steadfast to the lessons contained in this book and integrate them, the journey to healing will feel like moving downstream with the flow instead of an upstream fight against the current.

GOING WITH THE FLOW OF THE UNIVERSE VERSUS FIGHTING THE CURRENT

Heal Yourself: A Return to Wholeness

One of the greatest sources of suffering is fighting against the flow of the entire universe. We create more friction for others and ourselves by not accepting things as they are. Dr. Wayne Dyer used to say, "Trade in your expectations for appreciation." In life, we tend to have many expectations. We have expectations for others, our situations, and ourselves. And when those things don't happen according to our plan, we get angry, frustrated, and even depressed. Can you imagine how much you can reduce your suffering just by going with the flow of the universe?

Let's suppose you expect your child to go to college. To that end you start saving money toward his college education when he is a baby. Or perhaps you expect that he might get a basketball scholarship so you put him in basketball at age four. Then you pay for coaches and travel teams, only to have him tell you in his senior year that he doesn't plan on going to college. Because you have built up this dream for him, you get angry and upset when you hear *his* plans for his own life. In this example, what would be the cause of your suffering? It would only be your expectations.

Now let's explore another example that might hit closer to home. Many people get married expecting that the marriage will last forever. But reality says that over 50% of all marriages end in divorce. Let's suppose that one day your spouse announces to you that he or she wants a divorce. In your expectation to stay married forever, you let the information destroy you emotionally. Of course, disappointments come in all shapes and sizes. Hearing the devastating news that your marriage is ending can cause all sorts of emotions. However, believing that anything on this Earth will last forever is a false belief. The more you integrate the fact that the universe is going to flow the way it will flow, whether you get upset and uptight or not, will change your level of suffering. Going back to the divorce example, what if after your divorce you discover a hidden talent that had been suppressed by the comfort of your marriage. Or what if you find a new partner who is much more aligned with your values? It all goes back to that bigger picture. By flowing with the course of the way things are, you can begin to notice that you're an actor in the big theatrical production of life. Just as the actor wouldn't give the director the play by play, neither should you in order to remain in peace.

Go with the flow of the universe. Move gently down the stream. See where life takes you without fighting the flow.

CHOOSING SANITY OVER INSANITY

If the only constant is change, then change is where we need to get to when we re-emerge as our healed self. I like the expression, "The definition of insanity is doing the same thing time and again and expecting a different result." Affirm and reaffirm this expression, *In healing myself, today, I choose sanity.*

Recently I had a situation that woke me up to this reality. For years I've had to deal with a certain person who conjures up a lot of fear within me. This person is irrational, volatile, and controlling. In dealing with him I always get tense and sick inside. I know, without a shadow of doubt, that he will try and take advantage of the situation, try to intimidate me, and make my life more difficult. Yet, I must deal with him. In the past couple of years, the solution has been to ask a family member for help. This time I realized that by asking other people who are close to me for help, it was only creating more tension for everyone involved. The person in question would not only find ways to make my life more difficult, but also to instill fear in my other family members. In the midst of the stress and upon the advice of a dear friend, I made the decision to stop the insanity. I now have a new plan to put money aside to pay a neutral third party when I have to deal with this person at any time in the future.

Oftentimes we find ourselves in situations that cause us to repeat unhealthy patterns. Choosing sanity means finding a different pathway and then taking it.

DISCONNECT TO RECONNECT

Throughout the years of internet connection and depending on my service provider, I've often had problems with internet connectivity. One second I'm in the flow working and browsing and then, "boom!" the internet slows down or disconnects. If this has happened to you, I'm sure you know how frustrating it can be. Sometimes the connection comes back organically, but most of the time when I call my service provider the customer service representative says, "Turn off your router, wait ten minutes, then allow it to reboot." And when I do that, lo and behold, the internet is back on full force.

At times you'll find that if you don't disconnect from the world you'll have a hard time feeling whole. The pull toward following the crowd or the opinions of others, whether or not they're significant in your life, is strong. We all have people and responsibilities to take care of and it can be easy to forget to reconnect to your higher self.

Reconnecting to nature is the best way to put your life into perspective. Get outside and observe how nature acts and reacts. Put away your electronic devices while you recharge your battery. Take a social media break if you can. You will be surprised to learn that nothing will have changed in the time you're offline. Disconnecting allows you to stay in observation mode and get out of ego when you find you're too caught up in the daily grind.

NURTURING YOURSELF

If you're a caretaker or nurturer, you may have been accustomed to putting others' needs first. In becoming whole you must learn to nurture yourself first on a daily basis. Even if you're a mom or dad, your needs must come first. That includes exercising daily, eating properly, and making sure you take the time to nurture your friendships and relationships.

For many years I put my kids first and failed to pay attention to what I needed. For over a decade I didn't really buy myself clothes because it was all about the kids. In hindsight, that mentality was crazy. I was sending the message to my kids that my needs didn't matter. In addition, when I was married I did the same thing and ended up with a martyr mentality because each time I did ask my spouse for time away from the kids, I got big push back.

You count and you matter. But unless you believe it, you're going to have a difficult time convincing others of this truth.

SELF-ACCEPTANCE

Throughout this entire book we've focused on a return to wholeness. I've emphasized that healing is about the integration of your body, mind, emotions, soul, and spirit. However, do you find that you still have resistance about accepting every part of yourself?

To illustrate, let's start with the physical body. Many people have issues with total body acceptance. You probably hear it all the time. People utter phrases like:

I wish I were taller.
I wish I were thinner.
I wish I had more hair.
I wish my metabolism was faster.

Heal Yourself: A Return to Wholeness

I wish I looked younger.

Ever since I can remember, I've had body acceptance issues. I'm not sure why or how it started. Even though I'm not super heavy and never have been, I've had consistent problems keeping weight off. One time my mother showed me my third grade picture. I looked pudgy with big, fat cheeks. And instead of wearing a nice slim skirt for Girl Scout Brownies, I had to wear a jumper where you could see my stomach sticking out, like a pregnant lady. Around that time my mom also put me in ballet several days per week and that helped me become thin again. But I was always conscientious on how I looked and presented myself. Today people might look at me and think that I have never had a weight problem and that is because I pay attention *all the time*. I used to lament on how easy it is for some women to eat whatever they want and keep the weight off. In my envy, I would get angry or upset. I wanted so badly to be able to be carefree and not have to worry about putting on a few pounds if I let loose. But that's not the way my body operates. For some genetic reason my body tends to hold onto fat easily and efficiently. It's a constant uphill battle to maintain my weight. In recent years, I've learned to accept that my body works in a certain way and I just have to deal with it. I have to work harder at it every single day, but if I want to stay fit, I have no other choice. I might not think it's fair, but it's a life choice that I've made for my health and wellbeing.

You might not have weight issues. Maybe you wish you didn't have allergies. Or maybe you wish you had better facial features. Or perhaps your self -acceptance has nothing to do with your body at all. Maybe you wish you came from a different family with more supportive relatives. Whatever the case, wholeness comes with acceptance.

BELIEVE IN YOURSELF

Regardless of what the world thinks about you, you must believe in yourself. You are the only one who knows what's best for you. Self-assurance and self-confidence are the keys to attaining nearly everything in life. If you don't believe in you, who will?

In the movie, *The Big Sick (2017)* the character who play's Emily's mother (played by Holly Hunter) says a genius line. Emily, a young college student, is forced into a coma after having flu-like symptoms with complications that leave doctors baffled. In this scene, the boyfriend, Kumail, is saying to the mother that they must trust the doctors because they know exactly what they're doing. The mother responds, "No they don't. They're just winging it like the rest of us."

It's true. Even the so-called "experts" are just playing the same guessing game as you and me. It's human nature to want to put your life safely in someone else's hands. After all, that's what you did growing up and for the most part that turned out pretty well. Yet in doing so as an adult, you let go of belief in yourself and also put responsibility on someone else for your life.

I agree that we are interdependent as humans and we must be to survive and thrive. But if you're letting other people call the shots for your life because you're afraid to step out into the world with self-confidence and belief in your own abilities, you're missing the mark and will suffer for it.

BELIEVE IN YOUR WORTHINESS TO RECEIVE

As you re-emerge into the fullness of yourself, make sure you don't have any issues with receiving. Many people, especially the spiritually aware, have blockages when it comes to receiving. It's easy for them to give but not so easy to receive.

Can you imagine if you've been praying for healing and God is trying to answer your prayers but you don't believe in your worthiness to receive it? If you don't believe me, listen to the words that you and others might say when it comes to receiving. For example:

Oh no, I can't accept that gift it's too much.

Oh, let me pay. It's okay.

No, that's okay you don't have to come and see me, I'm fine.

I'm fine by myself.

You don't need to worry about me.

You don't have to pay me. I'm more than happy to do it.

Oh this dress? It's just an old thing I threw on.

All of those phrases show an inability to be able to receive. Let's explore how we can turn these around with a healthy ability to believe that you're worthy.

Thank you for the gift. I'm touched you would think about me.

Thank you for paying. It warms my heart.

Sure. I could use the company.

Having friends and family like you around makes me happy.

Thank you for thinking of me. How thoughtful.

Thank you for valuing my time. How about you pay for the materials and I'll give you half off the labor.

Thank you for complimenting me on my dress. It's my favorite one.

If you still have a difficult time feeling worthy to receive because of your upbringing or cultural education, here's a trick to learn.

Pretend that you're your own best friend or better yet, pretend that you are your child. In unconditionally loving your best friend or child, wouldn't you want them to receive the best? Wouldn't you want everything for them? As a loving person, you wouldn't want them to suffer. You would want them fed and nourished in body, mind, soul, and spirit. Is it possible that you would be upset if the person you loved the most didn't want to receive the gifts you were giving to them? You might get confused and hurt because you want so badly to love them and give them the world.

You are that person. Your Source loves you so much that he wants you to have everything. The way your Creator shows love for you is by giving you the world through other people and through life events. Receive those gifts with open arms. Prepare yourself to receive them. If healing is what you desire, you must keep your arms open to all of life's gifts. For healing itself is also a gift.

HONOR YOUR INNER WISDOM

When you are tuned into your inner guidance, you are infallible. One of the phrases I repeat often to my guardian Angels and to my higher power before a coaching session is, "Please help me to help this person and to get my ego out of it." You can ask for guidance to help you stay focused on your spiritual self in every aspect of life. The more you practice listening to your intuition, the stronger it becomes. Then the more validation you have of its truth, the more comfortable you'll be that your inner wisdom is accurate.

It is a positive feedback loop that starts with faith. Whenever I coach clients about romantic relationships I encourage them to listen to their inner guidance before they communicate with their significant other. Most who come to me for coaching are having a difficult time with their romantic relationship. So it stands to reason that the ego is probably getting in the way of proper loving communication.

Here's an example of how I lead them to making sure they're staying in spirit rather than ego.

When you're about to communicate with your partner in any way, ask yourself, *Am I acting or reacting out of ego or spirit? Am being manipulative in my speech or expecting a particular result? Am I judging or accusing my partner of not doing what I want? Or am I lovingly communicating with respect to his or her personality and life path?*

When you truly lead from your spiritual self in communication with others, less strife happens even if *they* are still operating from ego. Inner wisdom wants harmony. As you move through harmonious union with your higher self, the messages you receive will be aligned with your life path and with the flow of the universe.

Inner wisdom will sometimes not make logical sense. In fact, following your inner wisdom may even seem counterintuitive. But if you follow it enough, it will always be what you need. Remember, the sentiment you want more frequently is that of love and not fear. You want to consistently nourish love for yourself, others, and the world. If you find that you're operating more out of fear, you'll know that you're moving back toward ego-consciousness and suffering.

Your inner wisdom is trustworthy. In wholeness your inner wisdom is connected to the integral parts of you and also to the entire universe. In perfect flow, you'll know. Follow that knowing to your truth.

CHAPTER EIGHT: RECAP OF LESSONS LEARNED

1. Returning to wholeness is awakening to truth.
2. Operating from a sense of wholeness, with full awareness, takes time and patience.
3. One of the greatest sources of suffering is fighting against the flow of the entire universe.
4. Stop unhealthy patterns by choosing another path. Choosing sanity means finding a different pathway and then taking it.
5. Disconnect from daily life periodically to reconnect to your higher self and Source energy. Put away your electronic devices, get in touch with nature, and return to wholeness.
6. Accept every part of you, even the parts you don't like or wish you could change. Wholeness comes with acceptance.
7. Regardless of what the world thinks about you, you must believe in yourself. You are the only one who knows what's best for you.
8. Honor your worthiness to receive all that is good.
9. The more you practice listening to your intuition, the stronger it becomes.
10. In wholeness your inner wisdom is connected to the integral parts of you and also to the entire universe.

EPILOGUE

WHOLENESS AS A WAY OF LIFE

Hari Om, Om Tat Sat -Ancient Vedic Mantra (The manifest and unmanifest are both truth and therefore one.)

Wholeness is your natural state of being. Healing is also your natural state. As daunting as it may seem to maintain these states, you are never doing it alone. The entire universe has your back. Living from your spiritual self and moving back into the other layers in order to life fully, you'll realize that illness is an abnormal state. With time you'll be so accustomed to feeling well that when a bad feeling arises, it will feel foreign to you.

The constant way of wholeness requires balance. You must remain with one foot in the physical and the other in the spiritual at all times in order to honor and respect both sides. As you move through life in this way, people might think you're weird or eccentric. But you'll know if you're living in that balance because others will be drawn to your energy and your sense of peace.

Unusual is the person who lives in true balance and therefore true wholeness. Choose to be the outlier. You will then experience what it's like to be healed and free. Staying in the state of health provides a roadmap for others who want to attain it. Disease has become such the norm that your newfound recognition of absolute wellness, will defy the norm. Yet it is your human and divine right to claim perfect health.

As I finish this book in June 2020, I'm called to ask you to take on the task of wellness and healing for the collectivity. While your journey may have started with a personal goal to heal, as it continues your pursuit to living from your higher self will serve the world. The Earth and humanity are in great need of healing. As an individual who has learned the magic of healing through integration, you hold the key. You can now lead the way for others. Take great pride in it. I applaud you for being the anchor of light for others to follow. Be well.

ABOUT THE AUTHOR

Michelle S. Fondin has been teaching about health and wellness since 2008. She holds a Vedic Master certificate from The Chopra Center and is the author of nine published books including *The Wheel of Healing with Ayurveda* and *Chakra Healing for Vibrant Energy*. On her YouTube channel Michelle posts about health, wellness, spirituality, and romantic relationships. She does Angel readings, teaches yoga, and meditation. Michelle lives in the Los Angeles area in California.

CONNECT WITH MICHELLE FONDIN ON SOCIAL MEDIA:
  YouTube: https://www.youtube.com/c/Michelle-FondinAuthor
  Instagram: @michellesfondin

BOOK A COACHING SESSION OR READING WITH MICHELLE
www.fondinwellness.com

Made in the USA
Monee, IL
11 June 2023

35614606R00099